D1604143

OREGON NAMES

The Puzzlement of Pronouncing Names:

In California, for Salinas, it is said: <u>Sal-EE-nez</u>, but in Kansas, it is <u>Sal-EYE-nah</u>.

In Egypt, where the city is spelled C-a-i-r-o, it is <u>kEYE-roh</u>, but in Illinois, it becomes <u>K-roh</u>.

For Spokane, is it <u>spoh-kun</u>, <u>spo-KAIN</u> or <u>Spo-kan</u>? For those who know, it is <u>Spo-kan</u>.

For Yakima, is it <u>yaq-KEE-muh</u> or <u>YAK-em au</u>?

In Oregon, Estacada is <u>es-tuh-kay-duh</u> not <u>es-tah-KAH-dah.</u>

A native of the Oregon coast, who grew up around Florence, traditionally called it the <u>HECK-kah-uh</u> (Heceta) Head lighthouse although it was named for Bruno <u>hay-SEE-tuh</u>.

On the other hand, although it too is Spanish in origin, we say Cape <u>Blank-oh</u> – never <u>BLAHn-ko</u>. Also on the coast, is it <u>yah-CHATS</u> (Yachats) or <u>yah-hots</u> – pick the latter.

Astoria in Oregon gets <u>a-stohr-re-uh</u> while the district on Long Island in New York is <u>UH-stohr-re-uh.</u>

One does not want Senator Mark Hatfield's unique remark of nearly half-century ago to slip by us:

It seems that the then young Hatfield, many moons before be became a noted United States Senator, while talking to some students in the Beta Theta Pi Fraternity, in 1946, about proper pronunciation of a famous Oregon feature, the Willamette River, admonished his friends about calling it the "William-etty."

Senator Hatfield quipped that the name is easy to say if you just remember "it's *Will-AM-ette damnit* " !

And so it goes....

Oregon's Names;
How to Say Them ❓
And Where Are They Located ⬤

An Illustrated
Pronunciation Guide

Bert Webber, M. L. S.

WEBB RESEARCH GROUP
Publishers of Books About the Oregon Country

Published by:

WEBB RESEARCH GROUP PUBLISHERS
Books About the Oregon Country
P. O.Box 314 Medford, OR 97501 USA

There is **NO FAT** in this book.
Many publishers, in order to "thicken-up" a book, insert
blank pages between chapters and in the back of books.
FAT adds to the cost of the book.
The policy at Webb Research Group Publishers is to publish
"NO FAT" BOOKS.
This is one of them.

Library of Congress Cataloging-In-Publication Data:

Webber, Bert
    Oregon names, how to say them and where are they located? :
an illustrated pronunciation guide / Bert Webber
      p.   cm.
    Includes bibliographical references.
    ISBN 0-936738-72-3
    1. Names, Geographical–Oregon–Pronunciation. 2. English
language–Pronunciation–Dictionaries.   I. Title.
F874.W43   1995   92-33559
917.95'003–dc20   →Published 1995   CIP

Table of Contents

Map - State of Oregon	showing abbreviations	*vi*
Oregon County List	showing abbreviations	*vii*
Pronunciation Guide		*viii*
Introduction		9
Places starting with letter	A	14
	B	22
Southern Pacific Railroad Lines in Oregon (Maps)		28
	C	32
	D	40
Deadwood Covered Bridge (picture)		40
	E	44
	F	46
	G	48
	H	51
	I	55
	J	57
	K	58
	L	61
	M	65
Mount McLoughlin	(picture)	70
Mount Thielsen	(picture)	71
	N	73
	O	75
	P	78
	Q	82
	R	83
	S	87
Shimanek Covered Bridge (picture)		89
Sumpter Valley Dredge State Park (picture)		92
	T	94
	U	99
	V	100
	W	101
	Y	105
	Z	106
Bibliography		107
About the Author		109

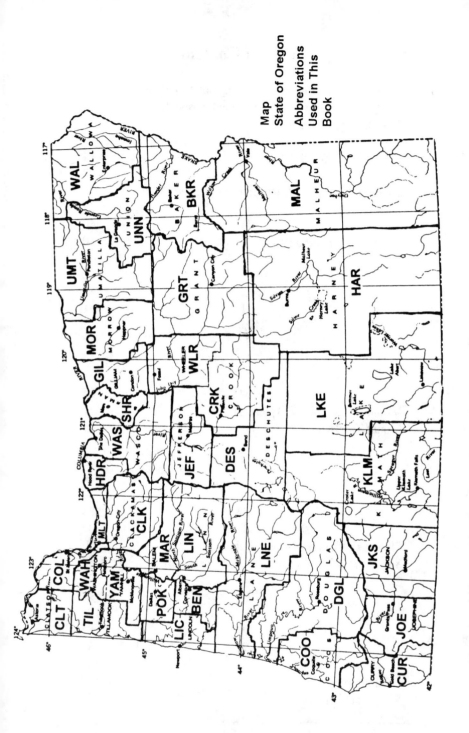

Map
State of Oregon

Abbreviations
Used in This
Book

Oregon Counties

No.	County	Map Code	Location - borders on
1.	Baker	**BKR**	NE - Snake River
2.	Benton	**BEN**	NW - Willamette R
3.	Clackamas	**CLK**	NW - Willamette Riv
4.	Clatsop	**CLT**	NW corner - Coast/Columbia R.
5.	Columbia	**COL**	NW - Columbia R.
6.	Coos	**COO**	SW Coast
7.	Crook	**CRK**	Center of state
8.	Curry	**CUR**	SW corner -Coast/California
9.	Deschutes	**DES**	Central
10.	Douglas	**DGL**	SW Coast
11.	Gilliam	**GIL**	Central - Columbia R.
12.	Grant	**GRT**	NE - Eastern
13.	Harney	**HAR**	SE - Nevada
14.	Hood River	**HDR**	NW - Columbia R.
15.	Jackson	**JKS**	SW - California
16.	Jefferson	**JEF**	Central
17.	Josephine	**JOE**	SW - California
18.	Klamath	**KLM**	S. Central - California
19.	Lake	**LKE**	S. Central - Nevada
20.	Lane	**LNE**	Central Coast/Willamette R.
21.	Lincoln	**LIC**	NW Coast
22.	Linn	**LIN**	NW - Willamette R.
23.	Malheur	**MAL**	SE - Idaho
24.	Marion	**MAR**	NW - Willamette R.
25.	Morrow	**MOR**	Central - Columbia R.
26.	Multnomah	**MLT**	NW - Columbia R.
27.	Polk	**POK**	NW - Willamette R.
28.	Sherman	**SHR**	Central - Columbia R.
29.	Tillamook	**TIL**	NW - Coast
30.	Umatilla	**UMT**	NE - Columbia R./Washington
31.	Union	**UNN**	NE - Blue Mts.
32.	Wallowa	**WAL**	NE corner - Washington
33.	Wasco	**WAS**	Central - Columbia R.
34.	Washington	**WAH**	NW
35.	Wheeler	**WLR**	NE - John Day R.
36.	Yamhill	**YAM**	NW Willamette R.

Pronunciation Key

a	as in	**a**pple c**a**t **a**dmit
ay	as in	**a**ce gr**e**y **A**pril b**a**y
ah	as in	t**o**p f**a**ther **a**rt
aw	as in	b**ou**ght s**a**w
e	as in	s**ai**d b**e**d b**e**tter
ee	as in	tr**ea**t s**ee** b**e**
er	as in	h**er** h**ur**t sm**ir**k
eye	as in	fl**y** m**i**ner s**i**ght
gh	as in	rou**gh** enou**gh** snu**ff**
i	as in	h**i**ll t**i**n w**i**sdom
oh	as in	s**ew** g**o** gh**o**st h**o**st
oo	as in	s**u**it Sio**u**x b**oo**t m**oo**n
ow	as in	h**ow** n**ow** br**ow**n c**ow**
you	as in	b**u**tte c**ue** m**ew** **u**nicorn
oi	as in	b**oy** j**oy** **oy**ster
00	as in	b**u**sh f**oo**t sh**ou**ld
uh	as in	**u**p l**o**ve t**ou**gh
zh	as in	citi**z**en **z**ither
hw	as In	**wh**o, **wh**at, **wh**y, **wh**en
j	as in	**j**ack **g**in **g**in**g**er
g	as in	**g**o **g**et **g**un
k	as in	**c**ake **c**ame **c**ome
s	as in	**c**igar **s**ell **c**entury
sh	as in	**su**gar **su**re **su**mac

Introduction

Where do these names come from?
        —Railroads, Mountains, People, Postoffices ....

Where are these places?
        —Well scattered over the surface of Oregon

While the place names found in Oregon come from a wide variety of sources, few are those who seem to realize that a great many of them are from the railroads.

Many of today's Oregonians know of two of these roads, the Union Pacific and the Southern Pacific. But there were and are a number of "short-lines" as well as other railroads in Oregon's colorful past.

The transcontinental AMTRAK and UP freights run the rails from Idaho to Portland, along with some branch lines. SP rolls freight trains and coastwise AMTRAK between Portland and California destinations as well as side-points. Historically, of the majors, there were The Oregon Short Line and the Oregon, Washington Railroad & Navigation Company (later the OR&N) as well as the Spokane, Portland & Seattle, The Great Northern Railway and The Northern Pacific. Many Oregon place names originated with the track-side sheds along the railroads. Every one of these sheds, be they manned switch-towers, telegraph offices, wayside passenger stalls, or mere telephone shacks, have names.

In the early days, the telephone shacks, about the size of a privy, were spaced quite close together, sometimes just a few miles apart. Names, names, names and more names were required. Some of these places were named for local people. "Adrian," on the Oregon Short Line, in Malheur County, is an example. Mr. James Adrian was a sheep rancher. Another is "Cruzatte," on the SP in Lane County, recalls Peter Cruzatte. He was a member of the Lewis and Clark Expedition. Another fellow was Daniel Curtain, who ran a sawmill. He fed business to the

SP. His name became a station and postoffice in Douglas County. And some foreigners were honored with a track-side name. One was "Airlie," for the Scottish Earl of Airlie.

There are names with religious background as "Dothan," (in Palestine, mentioned in the Bible) on the SP in Douglas County. "Enger," in Marion County, was the name of a local merchant. There was "Errol," a station on the Portland Railway Light & Power Company streetcar line, serving Errol Heights, a real estate development, in what is today southeast Portland. That name originated with a sailing ship.

Many names reflect Indian heritage. Others are words that describe the localities where they are. And many are from an arbitrary list made up by the railroads. "Acme" (Lane County) was one of these.

The names in Oregon were surely not limited to the needs of the railroads. "Glen," which operated in Lincoln County between 1894 and 1912, was to remember a local person's former out-of-state home town. "Frenchglen" (Harney County) was a combination name for land holdings of cattle ranchers. John Hobson provided his name for the postoffice of his salmon cannery, "Hobsonville," in Tillamook County.

Dr. Henry H. Hermann, a pioneer in Coos County, found his name on the "Hermansville" postmark. Pretty places, as "Pleasant Valley," in Baker County, are remembered. This was on the early O.W.R. & N. Railroad. "Scholls Ferry," in Washington County, was at the ferry dock on the Tualatin River. And there were joke or trick names. One was "Ragic" on the lower Rogue River. RAGIC is "cigar" spelled backwards! Another trickster was "Ekoms," also in Curry County. EKOMS is "smoke" spelled backwards.

Oregon's "Sisters" and "Brothers" are often mentioned. The two are in Deschutes County, about 45 miles apart, and are on the same road – Highway 20.

And so it goes....

The need for a book as this one has grown out of recognition that most folks who live in a place like to know how to pronounce that place's name. And other folks want to know where these places are located. For many decades, no such pronunciation guide book was available until Robert Monaghan's booklet in

1961. Bob Monaghan was the General Manager of the Oregon Association of Broadcasters as well as a professor in the University of Oregon's School of Journalism. His booklet was clearly intended for broadcasters as he wrote, "... from a professional broadcaster's point-of-view, correct pronunciation is necessary to clarity."

His objective was to steady the tongues of broadcasters when they were about to trip over a unique name. How about Yachats, Scappoose, Siuslaw, Umpqua, Heceta and Willamette – as a few? Today we have addeed Rajneeshpuram.

With the ever expanding number of television and radio stations today, and with the numbers of new "Broadcast School" graduates entering Oregon to work at reading the news, our ears reveal there is a demonstrated need – ah: demand – for a book demonstrating how to say the names of the places in Oregon. This book will save these fine folks from embarrassing themselves right there in front of a microphone, or TV camera, when it comes to pronouncing unique Oregon names properly.

But our book has really been created for the general public.

For this book, pronunciations suggested are based on the common traditional usage as tabulated after many reference sources were consulted (and a number of persons were asked). When several pronunciations turned up for a given name, we have selected what the majority suggested. This method guarantees that the final pronunciations appearing here are realistic. Of course, now and then there is a genuine split in opinions on how to say a name. When this happens, we show both and possibly add a few words about them.

There is a pronunciation guide in the front of the book.

Each name in the book is keyed to the county where it appears on a map – also in the front of the book.

In the "Location" column, to give directions clearly, we use compass arrows:

↖ northwest;   ↑ north;   ↗ northeast;   → east;
↘ southeast;   ↓ south;   ↙ southwest;   ← west.

When we refer to a highway, we use the highway number. If there was a post office at this place, past or present, we show 🏣.

Example:

 Blalock   BLAY-lahk   GIL   9 mi ← of Arlington. Hwy I-84

This is interpreted as being in Gilliam (GIL) County (cty) 9 miles (mi) west (←) of Arlington on Highway I-84. There once was a Post Office at Blalock.

Readers will note from this example that we include the location as well as the proper pronounciation.

The editor states however, this book is not intended as an elaborate listing of every place in Oregon – we have chosen those place names that seem to be the most difficult to pronounce – and the listing of place *locations*, important as they are, are secondary to properly saying the names.

Nevertheless, many of the locations are hard to find on common maps. We have tried to be helpful in an effort to assist readers, by locating many of these places. Again, as the book's purpose is to identify the more difficult names to *pronounce,* no effort has been made to provide place locations for the easier names basically omitted from the book.

Many of the name locations are in the mountains. For reader assistance, we cite the U. S. Geological Survey topographic maps for many of these sites in the "location" column throughout these pages. These maps are cited by name as: BONE SPRING TOPO.

For commercially produced maps, we referred to a number of Metzker's Maps, the earlier editions preferred, because many of these names have historical significance and many are no longer carried on modern maps. We were also fortunate in acquiring several official lists of railroad station names.

For some names, there are pertinent historical notes, the data not appearing in other sources consulted. For some folks, where visualizing names actually appearing on signs might be helpful to

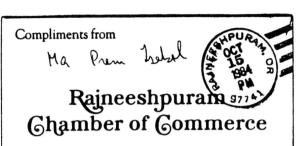

understanding them, we have included a few pictures of some signs. As a large number of the names were those used by Post Offices, many of our "signs" are reproductions of rare postmarks. We are indebted primarily to Leonard G. Lukens, an Oregon Postal Historian, who searched his collection then permitted us to use some of his postmarks here. Many of these imprints, from the discontinued offices, have never been shown in any book before.

As for determining where some places are located, should they not be included in this book, there are several primary sources. One is *Oregon Geographic Names.* Another is *Oregon Post Offices 1847 - 1982.* For the railroads, a number of the names are in *Stations West.* Another way is to consult the index along the margin of a current official highway map. Alas – even with these sources, all places in Oregon, including some that are on the main highways, are not easily identified. Our bibliography lists other books in which many of these places, and their stories, are included.

I am indebted to my colleague of many years, Richard J. Portal, Reference Librarian retired, now of Salem, Oregon, who scrounged for old maps for use on this project, and to the Reference Department staff of the Jackson County Library System, Medford, for assisting with the nit-picking needed for accuracy.

I am indebted to my wife, Margie, for her diligence with editing as well as for positive recommendations.

For exhaustive descriptions about many of the places in Oregon, we mention again Lewis L. McArthur's *Oregon Geographic Names.* (McArthur does not include pronunciations.)

Our book is recognized by the Library of Congress, and it

passes book selection criteria for use in schools and at Reference Desks in Public Libraries.

> Note: Since this book went into production, Southern Pacific Company, shown here as SPRR, has given notice that it intends to sell about 400 miles of trackage in Oregon to RailTex. The lines involved are primarily from Eugene to California and west, from Eugene, to the coast. This new business in Oregon will be known as The Central Oregon and Pacific Railroad. To retain continuity within this book and with older works, a number of which are in the bibliography, the RailTex lines are shown here as SPRR.

The compiler is aware that some folks may differ with some of the pronunciations included here. Letters of constructive criticism may be sent to the publisher whose address is on page iv. Whether personal replies can be provided will depend on the volume of work at the time correspondence is received.

Bert Webber
Master of Library Science
Central Point, Oregon

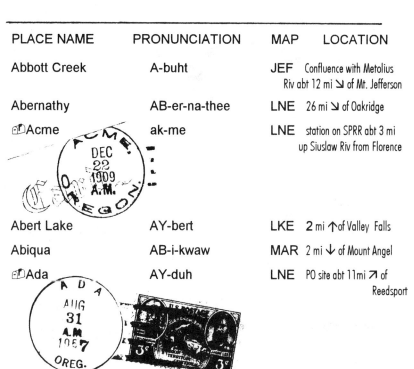

NOTE: There are many places in Oregon bearing the same root names. For examples, these include Castle Creek in Jackson County, Castle Creek in Klamath County, Castle Rock in Clatsop County, Castle Rock in Morrow County, Castle Rock in Malheur County. Another is Murphy in Josephine County, Murphy Bar in Polk County, Murphy Creek in Wallowa County, Murphys Camp in Tillamook County.   —The Editor.

Key to Standard Abbreviations For This Book—

abt - about	btwn - between	cty - county	Cr - creek
Hwy = highway	Lk - lake	mi - miles	Mt - mountain
nr - near	Pk - park	PDX - Portland	PO - postoffice
Riv - river	sta - station		

PLACE NAME	PRONUNCIATION	MAP	LOCATION
Abbott Creek	A-buht	JEF	Confluence with Metolius Riv abt 12 mi ↘ of Mt. Jefferson
Abernathy	AB-er-na-thee	LNE	26 mi ↘ of Oakridge
Acme	ak-me	LNE	station on SPRR abt 3 mi up Siuslaw Riv from Florence
Abert Lake	AY-bert	LKE	2 mi ↑of Valley Falls
Abiqua	AB-i-kwaw	MAR	2 mi ↓ of Mount Angel
Ada	AY-duh	LNE	PO site abt 11mi ↗ of Reedsport
Adair (Camp)	a-DARE	BEN	9 mi ↑ of Corvallis. Hwy 99W. This was a WW-II Basic Training Camp for the 96th and other Infantry Divisions
Adrian	AY-dree-un	MAL	12 mi ↓ of of Nyssa

15

PLACE NAME	PRONUNCIATION	MAP	LOCATION
✉Adel	ah-DEL	LKE	35 mi → of Lakeview
Ady	AY-dee	KLM	10 mi ↓ of Klamath Falls ✉
✉Agate	AG-uht	JKS	PO was 6 mi ↑ of Medford
✉Agness	AG-nes	CUR	On Rogue River at confluence with Illinois Riv abt 30 mi→ of Gold Beach
Ahalapam Cinder Field	ah-HAL-uh-pam	LNE	↑ of the Three Sisters mtns on Cinder Field the summit of the Cascade Range. *See* NORTH SISTER TOPO
✉Ahlers	Ah-lerz	CLT	PO was abt 12 mi ↘ of Seaside
✉Aims	AYMS↑	CLK	6 mi ↗ of Sandy
Ainsworth State Park	AYNS-werth	SHR	37 mi → of Portland. Hwy I-84
✉Airlie	AYR-lee	POK	abt 8 mi ↙ of Monmouth
✉Ajax	AY-jax	GIL	abt 3 mi → of John Day Riv and abt 12 mi ← of Condon
Akin	AY-kin	DGL	6 mi ↑ of Roseburg
✉Alamo	AL-am-oh	GRT	abt 6 mi ↙ of Granite
✉Albany	AWL-ban-ee	LIN	24 mi ↓ of Salem
✉Albee	AHL-bee	UMT	5 mi ↑ of Uktah
✉Albina	al-BEYE-nuh	MLT	District of PDX
Alco Creek (also Alcoe)	AL-koe	JKS	About 8 mi ↗ of Trail
Alder	AHL-der	WAL	abt 2 mi ↙ of Enterprise
Aldrich Point	AWL-drich	CLT	On Columbia River → of Tongue Point which is at → end of Astoria
✉Ale	AY-ul	MAR	PO at W.Stayton RR station abt 4 mi ← of Stayton
Alecs Butte	AL-ex	YAM	1 mi ↓ of Yamhill
✉Alfalfa	AAL-fal-fa	DES	PO site abt 15 mi → of Bend

16

PLACE NAME	PRONUNCIATION	MAP	LOCATION
📫Algoma	al-GOH-muh	KLM	abt 10 mi ↑ of Klamath Falls.

📫Alicel	al-i-SEL	UNN	abt 9 mi ↗ of LaGrande on Joseph Br of UPRR
📫Alkali	AL-kuh-leye	GIL	site was on ↓ bank of Columbia Riv former site of Arlington now flooded behind John Day Dam.
📫Allegany	al-uh-GAY-nee	COO	10 mi ↗ of Coos Bay
Allingham Camp and Guard Sta	ahl-ling- ham	JEF	Upper Metolius Riv area. Elev. 2,900 ft. See BLACK BUTTE TOPO
📫Allston	AWL-stuhn	COL	4 mi ← of Rainier. Hwy 30
📫Alma	AL-muh	LNE	on Siuslaw Riv abt 29 mi ← of Cottage Grove
📫Almeda	al-MEE-duh alternate pron: (al-MED-uh)	JOE	On Rogue Riv abt 25 miles ↖ of Grants Pass
📫Aloha	ah-LOH-huh	WAH	3 mi → of Beaverton
📫Alpha	AL-fuh	LNE	PO moved abt was finally nr 4 mi ↖ of Greenleaf
📫Alsea	ahl-SEE	BEN	abt 19 mi ↙ of Philomath
Alspough	AL-spow	CLK	1 mi ↓ of Eagle Creek
📫Altamont	AL-tuh-mahnt	KLM	1 mi ↘ of Klamath Falls
📫Althouse	ALT-hows	JOE	on Althouse Cr abt 4 mi ← of Holland
📫Alvadore	al-vuh-DOHR	LNE	10 mi ↖ of Eugene. Hwy 99W
📫Alville	AWL-vil	GIL	abt 8 mi ↖ of Condon

17

PLACE NAME	PRONUNCIATION	MAP	LOCATION
Alvord Peak	al-vohrd	HAR	elev. 7,132 ft. on Steens Mountain. *See* FIELDS TOPO
Amine Peak	AY-meyen	WLR	abt 11 mi ↙ of Clarno
⌖Amity	AM-i-tee	YAM	7 mi ↓ of McMinnville.
⌖Amos	AY-mohs	LNE	14 mi ↓ of Cottage Grove
Amota Butte	a-mah-ta	LKE	elev. 5,500 ft. *See* INDIAN BUTTE TOPO
Ana Spring	ANN-ah	LKE	abt 31 miles ↖ of Paisley. Hwy 31
⌖Anchor	AN-kohr	DGL	abt 7 mi → of Azalea on ↑ side of Galesville Reservoir

Alvord Peak	al-vohrd	HAR	elev. 7,132 ft. on Steens Mountain. *See* FIELDS TOPO
Amine Peak	AY-meyen	WLR	abt 11 mi ↙ of Clarno
⌖Amity	AM-i-tee	YAM	7 mi ↓ of McMinnville.
⌖Amos	AY-mohs	LNE	14 mi ↓ of Cottage Grove
Amota Butte	a-mah-ta	LKE	elev. 5,500 ft. *See* INDIAN BUTTE TOPO
Ana Spring	ANN-ah	LKE	abt 31 miles ↖ of Paisley. Hwy 31
⌖Anchor	AN-kohr	DGL	abt 7 mi → of Azalea on ↑ side of Galesville Reservoir

Aneroid Lake	ann-er-oid	WAL	in Walllowa Mtns. *See* HICKEY BASIN TOPO
Angell Peak	AYN-jel	GRT	at summit of Blue Mtns near junction of Baker, Grant, Union ctys. *See* ANTHONY LAKES TOPO
⌖Anidem	ANN-ee-dem	LIN	↓ of Gates on Quartzville Cr. *See* YELLOWSTONE MOUNTAIN TOPO
Ankeny Hill	ANN-ken -ee	MAR	10 mi ↑ of Albany.

PLACE NAME	PRONUNCIATION	MAP	LOCATION
Anlauf	ANN-lawf	DGL	6 mi ↑ of Drain. Hwy 38
Annie Creek/Spring	ANN-ee	KLM	in Crater Lake Nat'l Park
Antelope	ANN-tuh-lohp	WAS	Abt 8 mi ↓ of Shaniko.

Hwy 218. <u>NOTE</u>: Antelope was legally renamed <u>Rajneesh</u> for awhile, but the PO never changed its name. Later the name Antelope was restored. Antelope is nearest town to <u>Rajneeshpuram</u>. During the town's tenure as Rajneesh, newspaper and TV people often confused the two places frequently leaving impressions that they were one-and-the-same place which, of course, they were not being 18 miles apart. Refer to the location map under <u>Ranjeeshpuram</u>. *See* Bibliography

PLACE NAME	PRONUNCIATION	MAP	LOCATION
Anoka	ANN-oka	COL	on Pebble Creek abt 5 m ↓ of Vernonia
Anthony Lakes	ANN-though-nee	BKR/UNN	18 mi ← of North Powder on Forest Service Rd
Antoken Creek	an-TOH-ken	WAS	on Warm Springs Indian Reser, flows into Deschutes Riv.
Antone	an-TOHN	WLR	on Rock Cr abt 23 mi ↘ of Mitchell
Apiary	AA-pee-air-ee	COL	PO at bee farm abt 8 mi ↙ of Rainier
Applegate	A-pell-gayt	JKS	↙ of Jacksonville, Hwy 238
Arago	AY-ruh -goh	COO	abt 6 mi ← of Coquille
Arant Point	AY-rant	KLM	in Crater Lake Nat'l Pk
Arcadia	ahr-CAYD-dee-uh	MAL	7 mi ↓ of Ontario. Hwy 26
Arch Cape	ahr-ch	CLT	↓ of Cannon Beach
Ardenwald	ahr-duhn-wahld	CLK	2 mi ↑ of Milwaukie
Argenti	ahr-GEN-ty	MAR	abt 12 mi ↙ of Silverton
Arko	ahn-ko	WAL	nr Washington line abt 3 mi ↖ of Troy

19

PLACE NAME	PRONUNCIATION	MAP	LOCATION
🖂Arleta	ar-LEE-tah	MLT	neighborhood in →PXD

PLACE NAME	PRONUNCIATION	MAP	LOCATION
🖂Arlington	AHR-ling-tuhn	GIL	on Columbia Riv. Hwy I-84
Armet	ar-MET	LNE	btwn Lowell and Oakridge. Hwy 58
Armitage	ARM-i-tij	LNE	4 mi ↑ of Springfield
🖂Armin	AHR-min	WAL	abt 12 mi ↘ of Joseph
🖂Arock	AY-rawk	MAL	28 mi ← of Jordan Valley
Arrah Wanna	AHR-rah	CLK	1 mi ↓ of Wemme
Arrastra Creek	uh-RAS-trah	JKS	↓ of Talent off Hwy I-5
Arvard	AHR-vahrd	LNE	3 mi ↑ of Eugene
🖂Asbestos	as-BES-tuhs	JKS	↖ corner of cty nr Evans Cr. ↑ of Hwy I-5

PLACE NAME	PRONUNCIATION	MAP	LOCATION
Aschoff Buttes	ash-chawf	CLK	abt 5 mi → of Marmot Butte
🖂Ashland	ASH-land	JKS	about 11 mi ↑ of Calif. line, 12 mi ↓ of Medford. Hwy I-5
Aspen Lake	AS-pen	KLM	← of Upper Klamath Lake
🖂Astoria	as-TOHR-ee-uh	CLT	on Columbia Riv at

Young's Bay. Hwy 101. The district on Long Island in New York is pronounced uh-STOHR-ee-uh

PLACE NAME	PRONUNCIATION	MAP	LOCATION
🖂Athena	a-THEE-na	UMT	midway btwn Pendleton and Walla Walla. Hwy 37

PLACE NAME	PRONUNCIATION	MAP	LOCATION
Athey Canyon	A-thee	POK	abt 2 mi ↗ of McCoy
Attwell Creek	at-wel	HDR	nr Cascade Locks. Hwy I-84
🖂Audrey	AWD-rey	BKR	9 mi ↘ of Whitney
Augur Creek	AWG-er	LKE	↖ of Lakeview
Augusta Creek	uh-GUHS-ta	LNE	tributary of S.Fork MacKenzie Riv.
🖂Aurora	aw-ROHR-rah	MAR	abt 28 mi ↓ of PDX. Hwy 99E
Austa	AW-stuh	LNE	btwn Florence and Eugene. Hwy 128
Avalon Park	A-vuh-lawn	WAH	abt 4 mi ← of Tigard
Avery's	AY-ver-ees	BEN	First PO in cty was on ↑ bank Mary's Riv at confluence of Willamette Riv
Augusta Creek	uh-GUHS-ta	LNE	tributary of S.Fork MacKenzie Riv.
🖂Aurora	aw-ROHR-rah	MAR	abt 28 mi ↓ of PDX. Hwy 99E
Austa	AW-stuh	LNE	btwn Florence and Eugene. Hwy 128
Avalon Park	A-vuh-lawn	WAH	abt 4 mi ← of Tigard
Avery's	AY-ver-ees	BEN	First PO in cty was on ↑ bank Mary's Riv at confluence of Willamette Riv
Avon	AY-vahn	MLT	4 mi ← of PDX
Awbrey Mountain	AW-bree	JEF	elev. 5,431 ft. *See* FOLEY BUTTE TOPO
🖂Axtell	AX-tel	LIC	on Yachats Riv abt 6 mi → of Yachats
🖂Azalea	uh-ZAYL-yuh	DGL	13 mi ↑ of Wolf Creek. Hwy I-5

PLACE NAME	PRONUNCIATION	MAP	LOCATION

Baca Lake — BA-kuh — HAR ↓ of Malheur Lake near Donner and Blitzen Riv

🏚Bacona — bay-KON-nuh — WAH abt 7 mi ↘ of Vernonia

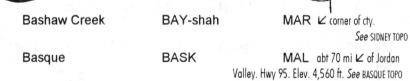

🏚Badger — BA-jer — SHR about 2 mi ↗ of Moro

🏚Baird — BERD — GIL in Alkali canyon elev. 750 ft. *See* SHUTLER FLAT TOPO

🏚Bakeoven — BAYK-uh-vuhn — WAS 8 mi ↖ of Shaniko

🏚Baker City — BAYK-er — BKR first known as Baker City, changed to Baker, changed back to Baker City. Hwy I-84 /US-30

Baldock Slough — BAL-dawk — BKR ↑ of Baker City

🏚Barlow — BAR-lough — CLK station of SPRR abt 2 mi ↘ of Canby

🏚Barnegat — BAR-nee-gat — TIL on Tillamook Spit. Name changed to BAYOCEAN, which town was totally innundated by coastal erosion. *See* biblio.

Bashaw Creek — BAY-shah — MAR ↙ corner of cty. *See* SIDNEY TOPO

Basque — BASK — MAL abt 70 mi ↙ of Jordan Valley. Hwy 95. Elev. 4,560 ft. *See* BASQUE TOPO

Bastendorff Beach — BAS-tuhn-dohrf — COO on ↓ side of entrance to Coos Bay

🏚Bates — BAYTS — GRT abt 1 mi ↘ of Austin

PLACE NAME	PRONUNCIATION	MAP	LOCATION
Battle Rock	BAT-ul	CUR	at Port Orford. Indian

battle in 1851. *See* biblio *Battle Rock Hero*. In WW-II, Japanese submarine safely hid on harbor's bottom but the US Navy, looking for the sub, didn't know it! *See* biblio for *Silent Siege-III*

☝Bayocean	bay-oh-shun	TIL	on Tillamook Spit.

Town, with large hotel, newspaper, school, many homes, washed into the sea due to coastal erosion starting about 1939, then narrow spit completely washed out in 1952. See bibliography

PLACE NAME	PRONUNCIATION	MAP	LOCATION
☝Beagle	BEE-gul	JKS	↖ of White City on Antioch Rd.
☝Beatty	BAY-tee	KLM	→ of Klamath Falls.
Beberg	BEE-berg	WAH	↓ of Beaverton
Belknap Crater	BEL-nap	DES	↑ of McKenzie Pass
Belle Passi	BEL-pass-ee	MAR	abt 1 mi ↓ of Woodburn
Bellrose	BEL-rohz	MLT	2 mi → of PDX
Bendire Mountain	BEN-deye-er	MAL	elev. 4,575 ft. *See* DEARMOND MOUNTAIN TOPO
Bencke Creek	BEN-uh-kee	CLT	near Jewell. *See* SAGER CREEK TOPO
Benemeer	BEN-uh-meer	WAH	abt 6 mi ↗ of Hillsboro
Benham Falls	BEN-uhm	DES	↖ of Lava Butte
☝Ben Holladay	*See* Holladay		
Benton County	BEN-tuhn	BEN	in ← Willamette Valley
☝Berkley	BERK-lee	LNE	slightly ↖ of Noti
☝Bethany	BF-thuh-nee	MAR	abt 1 ml ← of Silverton
Betzen	BET-suhn	LNE	abt 7 mi ↑ of Florence nr Mapleton on RR
☝Beulah	BYOO-luh	MAL	abt 15 mi ↑ of Juntura
Beusonic Heights	BYOO-sohn-ik	MLT	2 mi ← of PDX
Bieber Line Junction	BEE-ber	KLM	RR junction 1 mi ↓ of Klamath Falls
Billingslea Mountain	BIL-ings-lee	JOE	7 mi ↖ of Kerby. Elev. 4,169 ft. *See* TIN CUP TOPO

23

PLACE NAME	PRONUNCIATION	MAP	LOCATION
Bilyeu Creek	BIL-ee-oo	LIN	⬉ slope of Snow Pk.
			SEE JORDAN TOPO
🏛Binger	BIN-jer	DGL	upper Cow Cr valley abt
			11 mi ⬊ of Canyonville. Elev. 1,941. *See* CEDAR SPRINGS MOUNTAIN TOPO
Bingham Lake	BING-huhm	KLA	↓ of Crescent Lake.
			See COW HORN MOUNTAIN TOPO
🏛Birkenfeld	BER-kin-feld	COL	21 mi ⬉ of Vernonia.
			Hwy 202
🏛Bissell	BIS-sel	CLK	abt 10 mi → of Estacada
🏛Blachly	BLACH-lee	LNE	abt 3 mi ⬈ of Triangle Lk
🏛Blaine	bl-ayne	TIL	abt 7 mi → of Beaver on
			Nestucca Riv

Blakesley	BLAYK-slee	BEN	13 mi ⬉ of Corvallis
🏛Blalock	BLAY-lahk	GIL	9 mi ← of Arlington. Hwy I-84
Blanco (Cape)	BLAN-koh	CUR	6 mi ← of Sixes. Hwy 101.

The locals do not use the Spanish form BLAHN-koh which is being imported by Californians

Blazed Alder Butte	BLAY-suhd	CLK	elev. 4,120 ft.
			See BULL RUN TOPO
Blind Slough	BLEYEND	CLT	→ of Astoria on
			Columbia River
🏛Blodgett	BLAH-jet	BEN	17 mi ← of Corvallis. Hwy 20
🏛Blooming	BLOOM-ing	WAH	2 mi ↓ of Cornelius
Bloucher	BLOW-CHOHR	HDR	8 mi ⬋ of Hood River on RR
🏛Bly	BLEYE	KLM	abt 53 mi → of Klamath

Falls via Hwy 140; was ⬈ of Bly where Japanese bomb killed children in WW-II. *See* biblio for *Silent Siege-III*

24

-1945- 45th MEMORIAL ANNIVERSARY -1990-
BLY
MAY 5, 1990
OREGON
Joy Gifford, 13   Sherman Shoemaker, 11
Edward Engen, 13   Elsye Winters, 26
Joan Patzke, 13   Dick Patzke, 14
ALL KILLED BY JAPANESE BALLOON BOMB
NEAR HERE - WORLD WAR II

沈默の反撃

日本軍の米本土攻撃作戦記録

PLACE NAME	PRONUNCIATION	MAP	LOCATION
Blybach	BLEYE-bok	TIL	on Nehalem Riv abt 5 mi → of Mohler
Boardman	bohrd-mun	MOR	on Columbia Riv abt 26 mi → of Arlington. Hwy I-84
Boaz Mountain	BOHZ	JKS	elev. 3,461 ft. in ↓ part of cty. *See* RUCH TOPO
Bodie	B-OH-dee	UNN	was a RR siding elev. 4,025 ft. *See* HURON YOPO

Bohemia	Boe-HEEM-ee-uh	LNE	elev. 5,000 ft. *See* FAIRVIEW PEAK TOPO
Bolan Lake	BOH-luhn	JKS	abt 25 mi → of O'Brien
Bolivar (Mt)	BOH-li-vahr	COO	elev. 4,319 ft. extreme ↘ corner of cty. *See* MOUNT BOLIVAR TOPO
Bolton	BOHL-tuhn	CLK	↑ of Oregon City
Bonanza	buh-NAN-zuh	KLM	abt 25 mi → of Klamath Falls. Hwy 140
Bonifer	BOHN-i-fer	UMT	sta on UPRR → of Pendleton
Bonita	boh-NEE-tuh	LNE	abt 5 mi ↑ of Bohemia

25

PLACE NAME	PRONUNCIATION	MAP	LOCATION
Bonneville	BAH-nee-vil	MLT	on Columbia Riv 4 mi ← of Cascade Locks
Bosley Butte	BAHS-lee	CUR	elev. 3,432 ft. *See* BOSLEY BUTTE TOPO
Boswell Spring	BAHS-wel	DGL	abt 3 mi ↓ of Drain
Bourbon	BOOR-bohn	SHR	abt 7 mi ↓ of Grass Valley. Hwy 97
Bourne	BOHRN	BKR	abt 8 mi ↑ of Sumpter. Elev. 5,293 ft. *See* BOURNE TOPO
Bowdens	BOW-denz	MAL	abt 43 mi ↙ of Jordan Valley
Bowen	BOW-ehn	BKR	elev. 3,5109 ft. *See* BOWEN VALLEY TOPO
Bowlus Hill	BOW-luhs	UMT	↑ of forks in Walla Walla Riv. Elev. 2,080 ft. *See* BOWLUS HILL TOPO
Bowman Dam	BOW-man	CRK	on Crooked Riv, forms Prineville Res.
Boyer	BOI-yer	LIC	abt 8 mi → of Rose Lodge. Hwy 18
Bradley State Park	BRAD-lee	CLT	22 mi → of Astoria. Hwy 30
Bradwood	BRAD-wood	CLT	on Columbia Riv 26 mi → of Astoria
Braunsport	BRAWNS-pohrt	COL	abt 5 mi ↙ of Vernonia
Breitenbush	BREYE-ten-bush	MAR	abt 10 mi ↗ of Detroit
Briedwell	BRID-wel	YAM	2 mi ← of Amity. Hwy 99W
Bridal Veil (Falls/village)	BRID-ul-vayl	MLT	on Columbia Riv → of PDX
Brighton	BREYE-tuhn	TIL	nr mouth of Nehaem Riv ↑ of Tillamook. Hwy 101
Brightwood	BREYET-wood	CLK	abt 3 mi ← of Wemme. Hwy 26

PLACE NAME	PRONUNCIATION	MAP	LOCATION
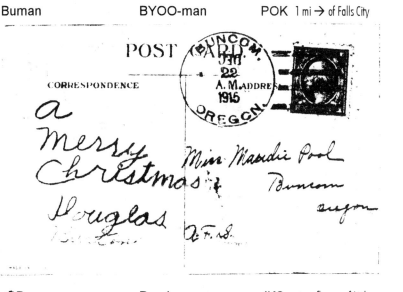Broadbent	BRAWD-ben-t	COO	↘ of Myrtle Point
Brophy Hill	BROH-fee	JKS	abt 2 mi → of Lakecreek.
Broughton Bluff	BRAW-tuhn	LNE	← of Elmira
Brower	BROW-er	MLT	2 mi ↘ of Bridal Veil
Bruin Run Forest Camp	BROO-uhn	CLK	4 mi → of Rhodendron
Brunner	BRUHN-ner	MLT	1 mi ↖ of Gresham
Bryant	BREYE-uhnt	CLK	abt 1 mi ↙ of Lake Grove
Buchanan	byoo-CAN-nuhn	HAR	abt 22 mi → of Burns. Hwy 20
Buell	BYOO-uhl	POK	abt 6 mi ↘ of Willamina
Buena Vista	boo-AY-nah-VIS-tuh	HAR	abt 19 mi ↑ of Frenchglen.
			Another Buena Vista is abt 6 mi ↓ of Independence in Polk cty
Bufo	BUH-FOH	DGL	abt 9 mi ↓ of Reedsport
Buford Creek	BYOO-fohrd	WAL	↑ of Flora off Hwy 3
Buman	BYOO-man	POK	1 mi → of Falls City

POST CARD
CORRESPONDENCE   A. M. ADDRESS
BUNCOM.
JAN
22
1915
OREGON

a Merry Christmas Douglas

Miss Maudie Pool Buncom oregon U.F.S.

Buncom	Bun-kum	JKS	at confluence of Little
			Applegate Riv and Sterling Cr. See McCREDIE SPRINGS TOPO
Bunyard Creek	Bun-yahrd	LKE	nr village of Silver Lake

27

PLACE NAME	PRONUNCIATION	MAP	LOCATION
Burchard	BER-chahrd	DGL	4 mi → of Scottsburg. Hwy 38
Burgess	BER-jes	BEN	2 mi ↓ of Corvallis. Hwy 99W
Burghardts Mill	BER-gahrts	CLK	abt 1 mi ← of Barton nr Clackamas River
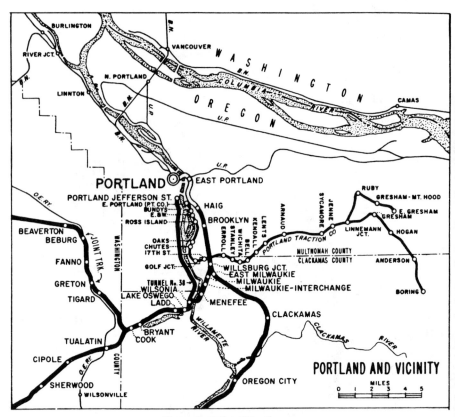Burkemont	BERK-mawnt	BKR	abt 20 mi ↗ of Baker City. Elev. 3,350 ft. *See* SAW TOOTH RIDGE TOPO
Burleson	BER-luh-suhn	LKE	abt 16 miles ↗ of village of Silver Lake
Byersville	BEYE-ayrs	YAM	abt 9 mi ← of West Chehalem

Trackside Stations
Southern Pacific Railroad - Lines in Oregon
Pages 28, 29, 30, 31

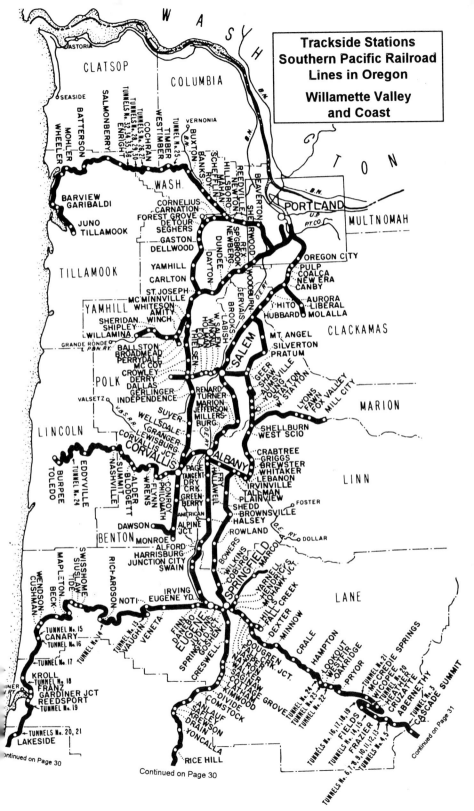

WASH

CLATSOP

COLUMBIA

ASTORIA

SEASIDE

BATTERSON
MOHLER
WHEELER

SALMONBERRY
TUNNELS N. 32, 34, 35, 36
TUNNELS N. 28, 29, 30
TUNNELS N. 26, 27
ENRIGHT

COCHRAN
TIMBER
WESTIMER
TUNNEL N. 25

VERNONIA

BUXTON
BANKS
SCHEFFLIN
ROY
HILLSBORO
NEWTON
REEDVILLE
SHERWOOD
SPRINGBROOK
REX
NEWBERG
WOODBURN
BEAVERTON

BN

PORTLAND
UP
PT CO

MULTNOMAH

BN

WASH.

CORNELIUS
CARNATION
FOREST GROVE
DETOUR
SEGHERS
GASTON
DELLWOOD

YAMHILL
CARLTON
ST. JOSEPH
McMINNVILLE
WHITESON
AMITY
WINCH

DUNDEE
DAYTON

OEN.

OREGON CITY

PULP
COALCA
NEW ERA
CANBY

AURORA
LIBERAL
MOLALLA

HITO
HUBBARD

BARVIEW
GARIBALDI

JUNO
TILLAMOOK

TILLAMOOK

YAMHILL

SHERIDAN
SHIPLEY
WILLAMINA

GRANDE RONDE
P&N RY.

BALLSTON
BROADMEAD
PERRYDALE
McCOY
CROWLEY
DERRY
DALLAS
GERLINGER
INDEPENDENCE

GERVAIS
LABISH
W SALEM
HOPMERE
TOGA
KEIZER
LANE
THELSEN

BROOKS

SALEM

MT. ANGEL
SILVERTON
PRATUM

GEER
SHAW
AUMSVILLE
YOUNG
W STAYTON
STAYTON

CLACKAMAS

CLARKS

POLK

VALSETZ

LINCOLN

CROWLEY
DERRY
DALLAS
GERLINGER
INDEPENDENCE

SUYER

RENARD
TURNER
MARION
JEFFERSON
MILLERS
BURG

WELLSDALE
GRANGER
LEWISBURG
CORVALLIS JCT.
CORVALLIS

V&S R.R.

SUMMIT
NASHVILLE
ALDER
BLODGETT

EDDYVILLE
TUNNEL N. 24

BURPEE
TOLEDO

SHELLBURN
WEST SCIO

LYONS
FAWN
FOX VALLEY
MILL CITY

MARION

ALBANY

PAGE
TANGENT
DRY CRK.
CONROY
GREEN
BERRY

FRY
HALWELL

CRABTREE
GRIGGS
BREWSTER
WHITAKER
LEBANON
IRVINVILLE
TALLMAN
PLAINVIEW

FOSTER

LINN

PHILOMATH
FLYNN
WRENS

DAWSON

MONROE

AMERICAN
ALPINE
JCT.

SHEDD
BROWNSVILLE
HALSEY

ROWLAND

BENTON

ALFORD
HARRISBURG
JUNCTION CITY
SWAIN

BOWERS
WILKINS
COBURG

DOLLAR

 O. P. RY.

SWISSHOME
SIUSLAW
TIDE

MAPLETON
BECK

WENDSON
CUSHMAN

RICH-
ARDSON

NOTI

IRVING
EUGENE YD.

MARCOLA

SPRINGFIELD

YARNELL
HENDRICKS
MOHAWK JCT.
FALL CREEK

LANE

TUNNEL N. 15
CANARY
TUNNEL N. 16

TUNNEL N. 17

TUNNEL N. 18

KROLL
FRANZ
GARDINER JCT.
REEDSPORT
TUNNEL N. 19

TUNNELS N. 20, 21
LAKESIDE

TUNNEL N. 13
VAUGHN

TUNNEL N. 14

VENETA

FINNBO
DANEBO
EUGENE
JUDKINS
SPRINGFIELD JCT.
GOSHEN
CRESWELL

DOUGREN
NAGEL
NAY
WALKER
SAGINAW
COTTAGE GROVE
LATHAM
KIMWOOD
DIVIDE
COMSTOCK
ANLAUF
SAFLEY
DREWSON
DRAIN

DEXTER

MINNOW

CRALE

HAMPTON

PRYOR

LOOKOUT
WESTFIR
OAKRIDGE

McCREDIE SPRINGS

WICOPEE
HEATHER
CRUZATTE
ABERNETHY
CASCADE SUMMIT

TUNNEL N. 21
TUNNEL N. 20
TUNNEL N. 3

TUNNELS N. 24

TUNNELS N. 22

TUNNELS N. 16, 17, 18, 19
TUNNELS N. 14, 15
FIELDS
TUNNELS N. 10, 11, 12, 13
FRAZIER
TUNNELS N. 8, 9
TUNNELS N. 6, 7
TUNNELS N. 4, 5

YONCALLA

RICE HILL

Continued on Page 30

Continued on Page 30

Continued on Page 31

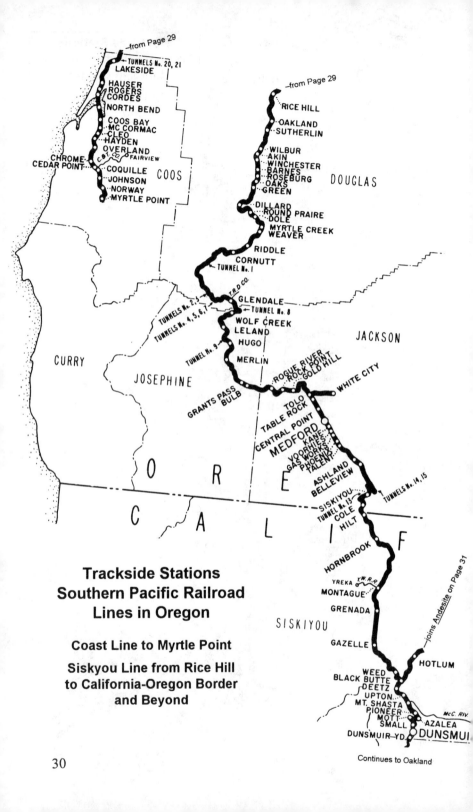

from Page 29
TUNNELS No. 20, 21
LAKESIDE
HAUSER
ROGERS
CORDES
NORTH BEND
COOS BAY
MC CORMAC
CLEO
HAYDEN
OVERLAND
FAIRVIEW
CHROME
CEDAR POINT
C.B.T. CO.
COQUILLE
JOHNSON
NORWAY
MYRTLE POINT

COOS

from Page 29

RICE HILL
OAKLAND
SUTHERLIN
WILBUR
AKIN
WINCHESTER
BARNES
ROSEBURG
OAKS
GREEN
DILLARD
ROUND PRAIRE
DOLE
MYRTLE CREEK
WEAVER
RIDDLE
CORNUTT
TUNNEL No. 1
T.R.D CO.
GLENDALE
TUNNEL No. 8
TUNNELS No. 2, 3
TUNNELS No. 4, 5, 6, 7
WOLF CREEK
LELAND
HUGO
TUNNEL No. 9
MERLIN
GRANTS PASS
BULB
ROGUE RIVER
ROCK POINT
GOLD HILL
WHITE CITY
TOLO
TABLE ROCK
CENTRAL POINT
MEDFORD
KANE
VOORHIES
GAS WORKS
PHOENIX
TALENT
ASHLAND
BELLEVIEW
SISKIYOU
TUNNEL No. 13
COLE
HILT
TUNNELS No. 14, 15
HORNBROOK
YREKA   Y.W.R.R.
MONTAGUE
GRENADA
GAZELLE
HOTLUM
WEED
BLACK BUTTE
DEETZ
UPTON
MT. SHASTA
PIONEER
MOTT
SMALL
AZALEA
DUNSMUIR YD.
DUNSMUI
McC. RIV.

DOUGLAS

JACKSON

CURRY

JOSEPHINE

O R E

C A L I F

SISKIYOU

Joins Andesite on Page 31

**Trackside Stations
Southern Pacific Railroad
Lines in Oregon**

Coast Line to Myrtle Point

**Siskyou Line from Rice Hill
to California-Oregon Border
and Beyond**

Continues to Oakland

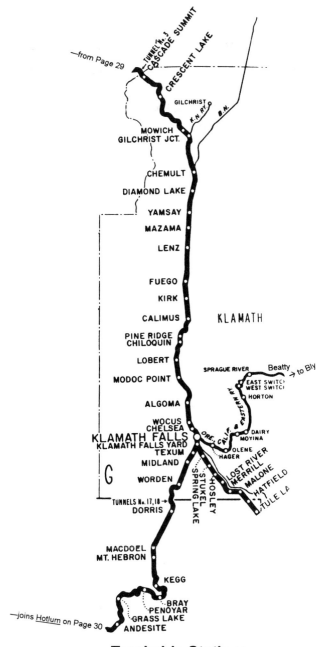

Trackside Stations
Southern Pacific Railroad - Lines in Oregon
Cascade Summit to California-Oregon Border and Beyond

Maps courtesy of Southern Pacific Company

PLACE NAME	PRONUNCIATION	MAP	LOCATION
Cache Creek	CASH	WAL	flows into Snake River at extreme ↗ corner of Oregon
Cahalin Spur	ca-HAL-uhn	WAH	3 mi ↓ of Tualatin
Cairo	KEYE-roh	MAL	short distance ↙ of Ontario at junction of Hwys 26 and 201
Calapooia River	kal-ah-POO-yuh	LIN	joins Willamete Riv at Albany
🏠 Calapooya	kal-ah-POO-yuh	LNE	abt 10 mi ← of Lebanon
Caldera	Kahl-DER-uh	DGL	5 mi ↓ of Roseburg
Calimus	KAL-i-muhs	KLM	siding on RR abt 30 mi ↑ of Klamath Falls
Calor	CAL-OHR	KLM	siding on SP RR at Calif. line
🏠Camas Valley	KA-muhs	DGL	↙ of Roseburg. Hwy 42
Cambrai	KAM-bray	WAS	siding on RR ↓ of Maupin
Cameron	KAM-ruhn	JKS	3 mi ↓ of Ruch (pron: Roosch) For details of all villages, post offices, families, of the Upper Applegate Valley, *see RUCH* in biblio
🏠Camp Adair	*see:* Adair		
Camp Alvord	Ahl-vord	MAL	Civil War outpost in Alvord Valley at → base of Steens Mtn
Camp Clatsop	*See* Clatsop		
Camp Maury	MOW-ree	CRK	30 mi ↘ of Prineville
Camp Namanu	nah-MAH-noo	CLK	3 mi ↑ of Boring
Camp Tsiltcoos (Siltcoos)	CHILT-koos	LNE	↓ of Florence. Hwy 101
🏠Camp White	Wh-yte	JKS	9 mi ↑ of Medford in Agate Desert. In WW-II the 91st Infantry Div trained here. For description of rugged army life there see biblio for *Camp White Oregon*
🏠Canby	KAN-bee	CLK	abt 9 mi ↓ of Oregon City. Hwy 99E
Canemah	kah-NEEM-uh	CLK	now the ↓ part of Oregon City at Willamette Falls.

32

PLACE NAME	PRONUNCIATION	MAP	LOCATION
Canton Creek	KAN-tahn	DGL	area to the ↑ of Roseburg
Cape Arago	see: Arago		
Cape Blanco	see: Blanco		
Cape Ferrelo	fer-RELL-oh	CUR	5 mi ↑ of Brookings.
Cape Kiwanda	KY-wahn-duh	TIL	1 mi ↑ of Pacific City
⌂Cape Meares (Also spelled Mears)	MEERS	TIL	8 mi ← of Tillamook at ↓ end (base) of Tillamook Spit
Cape Perpetua	per-PET-choo-uh	LIC	2 mi ↓ of Yachats. Hwy 101
Cape Sebastian	suh-BAS-tee-uhn	CUR	10 mi ↓ of Gold Beach.
Carberry Creek and camp	KAHR-ber-ee	JKS	btwn 2 and 3 mi → of
Carcus Creek	KAHR-kus	COL	slightly ← of Apiary
⌂Carus	KAHR-uhs	CLK	abt 7 mi ↓ of Oregon City nr Beaver Cr. Hwy. 213.
⌂Cascade Locks	kas-KAYD	HDR	on Columbia Riv abt 3 mi → of Bonneville Hwy I-84
⌂Cascadia	kas-KAY-dee-uh	LIN	abt 12 mi → of Foster. Hwy 20
Cason Canyon	KAY-suhn	GIL	↙ of Condon
Cathcart Place	kath-KAHRT	MAL	elev. 5,020 ft. See RAWHIDE SPRINGS TOPO
Cathlamet Bay	kath-LAM-muht	CLT	→ of Tongue Point
⌂Caviness	KAV-ee-nes	MAL	abt 15 mi ← of Brogan and abt 8 mi ↘ of Ironside
Cavitt Creek	KA-vit	DGL	abt 20 mi → of Roseburg
⌂Cayuse	KEYE-yoos	UMT	abt 11 mi → of Pendleton on the UPRR
⌂Cazadero	kaz-uh-DER-oh	CLK	abt 4 mi ↙ of Estacada
Cedar Camp	SEE-der	MAL	19 mi ↘ of Silverton

PLACE NAME	PRONUNCIATION	MAP	LOCATION
🏠Celilo	suh-LEYE-loh	WAS	12 mi → of The Dalles on the Columbia Riv. Hwy I-84

PLACE NAME	PRONUNCIATION	MAP	LOCATION
Cerro Gordo	SER-roh-GHOR-dough	LNE	6 mi → of Cottage Grove
🏠Champoeg	sham-POO-ig	MAR	on ↓ bank of Willamette Riv abt 3 mi ← of Butteville
Chaparral Creek	shap-uh-REL	WAL	flows into Minam Riv
Chapin Creek	CHAP-in	MOR	abt 6 mi ↓ of Hardman Ghost town. Hwy 207
Charbonneau	char-bow-kno	CLK	nr Wilsonville. Hwy I-5
Charlton	K-ARYL-tuhn	COL	on Columbia Riv ↓ of Goble
Chaski Bay	CHAS-kee	KLM	within Crater Lake in the National Park
Chatfield	CHAT-feeld	WAS	siding on UPRR on Columbia Riv nr Mosier → of Hood River
Cheeney Creek	CHEE-nee	CLK	is ↓ of Welches. Hwy 26
🏠Chehalem	chuh-HAY-lem	YAM	abt 5 mi ↗ northeast of Newberg. Hwy 99W
Chehulpum Creek	chuh-HUHL-pum	MAR	↗ of Jefferson
Chelsey	CHEL-see	KLM	4 mi ↑ of Klamath Falls. Hwy 97
🏠Chemawa	chuh-MAW-wuh	MAR	4 mi ↑ of Salem
🏠Chemult	shuh-MUHLT	KLM	abt 75 mi ↑ of Klamath Falls, mid-way to Bend, is 4,758 elev., gets a lot of snow. Hwy 97

34

PLACE NAME	PRONUNCIATION	MAP	LOCATION
Chenoweth	CHEN-oh-with	WAS	a district of The Dalles 1 mi ← of downtown. Hwy I-84
⌗Chesher	ches-eyer	LNE	on Long Tom Riv nr Noti
⌗Cheshire	ches-eye-r	LNE	sta on SPRR abt 7 mi ↓ of Monroe. Hwy 99W
Chesnimnus Creek	ches-NIM-nuhs	WAL	abt 8 mi ↖ of Imnaha
⌗Chetco	CHET-koh	CUR	was near mouth of Chetco

Riv then moved to nr mouth of Winchuck Riv. immediately ↑ of California line. Hwy 101

⌗Chewaucan	she-WAW-can	LKE	abt 5 mi ↓ of Paisley. Hwy 31
⌗Chico	CHEE-koh	WAL	abt 15 mi ↘ of Flora.
⌗Chiloquin	CHIL-uh-kwin	KLA	abt 23 mi ↑ of Klamath Falls. Hwy 97
Chinchalo	chin-CHAY-loh	KLA	siding on SPRR abt 19 mi → of Chemult
Chinidere Mountain	CHIN-i-deer	HDR	← of Wahrum Lake
Chinook Bend	chi-NOOK	LIC	↑ of Kernville. Hwy 101
Chinquapin	CHINK-uh-pin	JKS	in ↘ area of cty
Chocktoot Creek	CHAWK -toot	LKE	flows into Sycan Marsh
Choptie Prairie	CHOP-tee	KLA	btwn Saddle Mt and Chiloquoin Ridge
Chucksney	CHUHK-snee	LNE	abt 12 mi ↑ of Waldo Lake
Cipole	SEYE -pohl	WAH	btwn Sherwood and Tualatin.
⌗Clackamas	KLA-kuh-muhs	CLK	btwn Milwaukie and Oregon City
⌗Clarnie	KLAR-nee	MLT	siding on UPRR abt 5 mi ← of Fairview nr ↗ PDX city limits
⌗Clarno	KLAHR-noh	WLR	ghost town on John Day

Riv abt 20 mi → of Antelope. Hwy 218

PLACE NAME	PRONUNCIATION	MAP	LOCATION
⌂Clatskanie	KLATS -kuh -neye	COL	nr Columbia Riv 17 miles ← of Rainier. Hwy 30
⌂Clatsop	KLAT-sop	CLT	↓ of Warrenton. Hwy 101.

The Oregon National Guard operates a training camp renamed Capt Rilea abt 1 mi ↓ of the site of the Camp Clatsop RR station

Claxtar	KLAX-ter	MAR	station on old Oregon Electric RR ↑ of Salem
Cleawox Lake	KLEE-uh-wawx	LNE	abt 2 mi ↓ of Florence in the sand dunes.
Cleo	KLEE -oh	COO	railroad siding abt 2 mi ↓ of Coos Bay
⌂Cleone	KLEE-oh-nee	MLT	about 2 mi ← of Troutdale
⌂Clifton	KLIF -tuhn	CLT	on Columbia Riv abt 9 mi ↖ of Westport. Hwy 30
Coalca	koh-AL-koh	CLK	5 mi ↑ of Canby
Coaledo	koh-LEE-doh	COO	on Beaver Slouggh nr Coquille
⌂Cochran	KAHK-ruhn	WAH	siding on RR abt 28 mi ↖ of Forest Grove
⌂Colestin	KOHL-steen	JKS	abt 12 miles ↓ of

Ashland on a narrow dirt road abt alongside SPRR 3 mi ↑ of Calif. line

Concomly	kawn-KAWM-lee	MAR	station on Oregon Electric RR abt 3 mi ↘ of Gervais. Hwy 99E
⌂Condon	KAHN -duhn	GIL	abt 8 mi ↓ of Arlington
⌂Connell	KAHN-uhl	WAH	14 mi ↓ of PDX

36

PLACE NAME	PRONUNCIATION	MAP	LOCATION
Connoway	KAHN-noh-way	HDR	6 mi ↓ of Hood River
Conser	KAHN -ser	LIN	abt 5 mi ↑ of Albany
Contorta Point	kuhn-TOHR-tuh	KLM	on ↘ shore of Crescent Lake
Conyers Creek	KAHN-yers	COL	↓ of Clatskanie
Coombs	KOOMS	UMT	10 mi ↙ of Pendleton
Coopey Falls	KOOP-ee	MLT	nr Bridal Veil
✉Coos Bay	KOOS BAY	COO	city and bay Hwy 101
✉Coquille	koh-KEEL	COO	abt 18 mi ↘ of Coos Bay. Hwy 42
✉Corbett	KOHR-bet	MLT	20 mi ↘ of Portland
Cordes	KOHR-dez	COO	abt 3 mi ↑ of North Bend
✉Cornelius	kohr-NEE-lee-yuhs	WAH	abt 3 m ← of Hillsboro. Hwy 8
✉Cornucopia	kohr-nuh-KOH-pee-uh	BKR	abt 12 mi ↑ of Halfway

PLACE NAME	PRONUNCIATION	MAP	LOCATION
Cornutt	KOHRN-uht	DGL	abt 4 mi ↙ of Riddle
Corral Creek	kohr-RA-L	CLK	3 miles → of Wilsonville
✉Corvallis	kohr-VAL-lis	BEN	On Willamette Riv 9 ml ↙ of Albany. Hwy 99W/34
Cosmos	KAHS-mohs	LNE	5 mi → of Swisshome
Cosper Creek	KAH-sper	YAM	See GRAND RONDE TOPO
✉Cottrell	kaht-TREL	CLK	5 mi ↗ of Boring
Couse Creek	cows	UMT	joins Walla Walla Riv ↘ of Milton-Freewater
Coxcomb Hill	KAWX-KOHM	CLT	in city of Astoria upon which is the Astor Tower

PLACE NAME	PRONUNCIATION	MAP	LOCATION
⌂Coyote	keye-OH-tee	MOR	3 mi → of Boardman
Cozad Mountain	KOH-zad	DGL	↗ of Oakland
Cozine Creek	KOH-zeen	YAM	flows through McMinnville
Crale	KRAYL	LNE	station on RR ↘ se of Lowell
⌂Crater Lake	KRAY-tehr	KLM	elev. 6,176 ft (at lake).

See CRATER LAKE EAST TOPO. Visitors viewpoint at rim about 8,000 ft. elev. A seasonal PO, presently in the Headquarters Bldg., is the highest elev. PO in Oregon.

CRESWELL DEC 14 11 AM 1959 OREG.

CRATER LAKE SEPT. 5 9 A.M. 1934 OREGON

PLACE NAME	PRONUNCIATION	MAP	LOCATION
Crates	krayts	WAS	on Columbia Riv 3 mi ↖ of The Dalles. Hwy I-84
⌂Creede	kree-dee	JKS	abt 5 mi ↗ of Medford
⌂Creswell	kress-wehl	LNE	town on Hwy I-5 abt 7 mi ↓ of Eugene
⌂Criterion	kreye-TIR-ee-uhn	WAS	abt 12 mi ↓ of Maupin
Critenden	Kritt-en-duhn	CUR	early name for Lakeport. *See* Floras Lake for details
⌂Croston	KROS-tuhn	MAR	on → bank of Willamette Riv abt 8 mi ↓ of Salem
⌂Cruzatte	KROO-zet	LNE	station on SPRR abt 22 miles → of Oakridge
Cucamonga Creek	koo-kuh-MUHN-guh	HAR	flows down ↖ slope of Steens Mtn.
Cullaby Lake	KUHL-uh-bee	CLT	a few mi ↓ of Warrenton nr Hwy 101
Cumley Creek	KUHM-lee	LIN	nr Detroit Dam
⌂Cumtux	kum-tucks	CUR	proposed postoffice site on Rogue Riv nr Agness
Cupper Creek	KOO-per	GRT	in nw corner of cty but flows s into John Day Riv

PLACE NAME	PRONUNCIATION	MAP	LOCATION
Currin	KER-in	LNE	abt 4 mi → of Cottage Grove
⊡Currinsville	KER-inz-vill	CLK	abt 2 mi ↖ of Estacada
⊡Curtin	KERT-n	DGL	abt 7 mi ↗ of Drain. Hwy I-5
Curry	KER-ray	CUR	most ↙ cty in Oregon, was

only place in continental U.S. to be bombed by Japanese airplane in WW-II strarting a forest fire. *See* biblio for *Silent Siege III*

⊡Cushman	KOOSH-muhn	LNE	on ↑ bank of Siuslaw
			Riv abt 4 mi → of Florence

PLACE NAME	PRONUNCIATION	MAP	LOCATION
Dabney State Park	DAB-nee	MLT	4 miles → of Troutdale.
Dairy	DAIR-e	KLM	abt 14 mi → of Klamath falls at junction Hwys 70/140
Dallas	DAL-uhs	POK	abt 15 mi ← of Salem
Dalreed Butte	DAHL-reed	MOR	on ← side of cty abt 2 mi ↑ of Willow Creek
Damascus	duh-MAS-kuhs	CLK	abt 9 mi ↘ of PDX
Damon Creek	DAMUHN	GRT	flows into the John Day Riv from ← of Mt. Vernon
Danebo	DAY-nuh-boh	LNE	4 mi ↖ of Eugene
Dant	DANT	WAS	abt 10 mi ↓ of Maupin
Daphne Creek Camp	DAF-nee	COO	on Forest Service Road abt 16 miles ↓ of Powers
Dardanelles	dahr-den-ELS	JKS	nr ↓ side of Rogue River across from Gold Hill. Hwy I-5
Davin Spring	DAVIN	CRK	abt 6 mi → of Paulina
Dayton	DAY-tuhn	YAM	abt 21 mi ↑ of Salem.
Dayville	DAY-VIL	GRT	at mouth of ↓ Fork John Day Riv
Deadwood	dehd-wud	LNE	on Deadwood Creek at

the Deadwood covered bridge abt 5 mi ↑ of Swisshome. Refer to *Oregon Covered Bridges. See* biblio.

40

PLACE NAME	PRONUNCIATION	MAP	LOCATION
⌂Deady	DEE-dee	DGL	4 mi ↓ of Sutherlin
Deford	DEH-fohrd	MAL	abt 6 mi ↗ of Follyfarm nr border with Harney Cty Hwy 78
Dehlinger	DIL-in-jer	KLM	13 mi ↘ of Klamath Falls
⌂Delake	dee-LAYK	LIC	district in Lincoln City. Hwy 101
⌂Delena	duh-LEE-nuh	COL	abt 17 mi ← of Rainier
Dellmoor	DEL-moor	CLT	abt 3 mi ↑ of Gearhart
⌂Del Norte	del-NOHRT	HAR	site is abt 3 mi ↖ of

Crane. Hwy 78. The pronunciation is a hard sound, "NORT" the same as Del Norte County in California. The Spanish 'Nor-tay' is used only by non-locals.

| Delura Beach Rd | del-OO-ruh | CLT | btwn Warrenton and |

Gearhart. On June 21, 1942, in WW-II, the Japanese Navy shot at nearby Fort. Stevens, one of the shells crashing 125 feet ← of intersection with Military Rd noted by historical marker. See biblio for *Silent Siege*

| Dement Creek | dee-MENT | COO | tributary of South Fork Coquille River |
| ⌂Denio | dee-NEYE-oh | HAR | on Nevada line abt 22 mi ↓ of Fields |

⌂Denzer	DEN-zer	LIC	on Lobster Cr, abt 5 mi ↘ of Tidewater which is → of Waldport
⌂Depoe Bay	DEE-pough	LIC	Hwy 101
⌂Deschutes	duh-SHOOTS		station on RR btwn Bend and

Redmond also name for cty, former postoffices in various locations such as at Sherars Bridge

Despain Gulch	DES-puhn	UMT	→ of Hermiston
⌂Detroit	dee -TROIT	MAR	on Santiam Riv. Hwy 22
Dever	DEEV -er	LIN	abt 6 mi ↑ of Albany
Devitt	DEV-it	BEN	on Mary's Riv abt 2 mi ↖ of Blodgett
Devore	de-VOHR	DGL	abt 2 mi ↑ of Yoncalla

PLACE NAME	PRONUNCIATION	MAP	LOCATION
Diablo Mountain	dee-AH -bloh	LKE	→ of ↑ end of Summer Lake
⌂Dillard	DIL-luhrd	DGL	abt 9 mi ↓ of Roseburg.
⌂Dilley	DIL-ee	WAH	station on SPRR abt 2 mi ↓ of Forest Grove
Dimmick	DIM-ik	JOE	abt 2 mi ↑ of Grants Pass
Dinca	DIN-kuh	UMT	abt 19 mi ↓ of Ukiah. Hwy 395
Dinwiddie Valley	DIN-wid-dee	LIN	↙ of Brownsville. See INDIAN HEAD TOPO

PLACE NAME	PRONUNCIATION	MAP	LOCATION
⌂Disston	DIS-tahn	LNE	abt 5 mi → of Culp Cr
Doane Lake	DOHN	POK	abt 2 mi ↙ of Willamina
Dodson	DAWD-suhn	MLT	rail siding ← of Warrendale.
Dominic	DAH-muh-nik	MAR	on RR ↗ of Mt. Angel
Donaca Lake	DAHN -uh -kuh	LIN	↓ of Detroit
Donner und Blitzen River	DAHN-ner uhn-blit-zen	HAR	empies into Malheur Lk. Riv is across Hwy 205 from Frenchglen
⌂Dorena	doh-REEN-uh	LNE	was indudated by Dorema Reservoir. Moved abt 2 mi ↖ of Culp Cr
Dosch Road	DAWSH	MLT	btwn Green Hills and Hillsdale
⌂Dothan	DOH-thuhn	DGL	sta and postoffice in Cow Cr canyon abt 10 mi ↖ of Glendaler on SPRR

PLACE NAME	PRONUNCIATION	MAP	LOCATION
⌂Dotyville	DAY-TEE-vil	LIN	site was abt 4 mi se of Scio
Dougherty Slough	DOHR-er-tee	TIL	abt 1/2 mi ↑ of Tillamook.
Doughly Creek	DOH-tee	TIL	mouth just ↑ of Kilchis Pt

42

PLACE NAME	PRONUNCIATION	MAP	LOCATION
Dougren	DOW-gruhn	LNE	station on SPRR ← of Dexter
⌂Dover	DOH-ver	CLK	postoffices moved a lot, was btwn 4 and 6 mi ↓ of Sandy
Dovre Peak	DOH-ver	TIL	in → part of cty
⌂Drewsey	DROO-zeə	HAR	abt mid-way btwn Juntura and Buchanan. Hwy 20
Drury Creek	DROO-ree	LNE	← of McKenzie Bridge
⌂Dryden	DREYE-duhn	JOE	abt 4 mi → of Selma
⌂Dufur	DOO-fer	WAS	abt 12 mi ↘ of The Dalles.
Dukes Valley	DOOKS	HDR	abt 9 mi ↓s of Hood River
⌂Dundee	DUHN-dee	YAM	abt 3 mi ↙ of Newberg on Hwy 99W
Durbin	DER-buhn	MAR	siding on RR abt 6 mi → of Salem
Durham	Der-uhm	WAH	immed ← of Hwy I-5 at DURMAN EXIT, the town abt 1 mi ← of Lake Grove, the community around the ← end of Oswego Lake
⌂Durkee	DER-kee	BKR	on Durkee Cr near confluence w/Burnt Riv abt 32 mi ↘ of Baker City. Hwy I-84
Duwee Canyon	DEW-ee	KLM	within Crater Lake Nat'l Park, canyon full of weird pinnacles along → side of road climbing steeply toward lake's rim.
Dyar Rock	DEYE-er	KLM	on ↓ rim of Crater Lake

43

PLACE NAME	PRONUNCIATION	MAP	LOCATION
Eby	E-bee	CLK	abt 5 mi ↘ of Canby
🏤Eckley	EKLEE	CUR	→ upper end of Sixes Riv abt 6 mi ↙ of Rural
🏤Ecola	ee -KOH -luh	CLT	PO site is in city of Cannon Beach nr mouth of Elk Cr.
Eddeeloe Lakes	ee-D-loh	LNE	↑ of Waldo Lake
🏤Edenbower	EE-den-BOWER	DGL	abt 2 mi ↑ of Roseburg. Hwy I-5
Eel Creek Forest Camp	EEL	COO	7 mi ↑ of North Bend
🏤Egli	eg-LEE	HAR	present name for the 3-bldg desert village of Wagontire abt 25 mi ↙ of Riley. Hwy 395
🏤El Dorado	el-duh-RAW-doh	MAL	a mining camp abt 2 mi ↖ of Malheur City, abt 10 mi ↗ of Ironsides
Eldriedge Bar	EL-drij	MAR	on Willamette Riv abt 3 mi ↑ of Wheatland
🏤Elgarose	EL-guh-rohz	DGL	abt 3 mi ↖ of Melrose
🏤Elkhorn	EL-KOHRN	DGL	in ↖ area of cty
🏤Elmira	el-MEYE-ruh	LNE	13 mi ← of Eugene on Fern Lake Reser
Elmonica	el-MWN-i-kuh	WAH	3 mi ↖ of Beaverton
Elmore Beach	ELMOHR	TIL	abt 1 mi ↓ of Rockaway.
Elowah Falls	e-LOW-ah	MLT	on McCord Creek → of PDX
Elrus	EL-ruhs	LNE	station on SPRR abt 15 mi ← of Eugene
🏤Elsie	EL-see	CLT	abt 6 mi ↓ of Jewel
🏤Ely (Elyville)	EE-lee	CLK	district within Oregon City on its ↓ side
🏤Embody	EM-bah-dee	LKE	abt 16 mi ↖ of village of Silver Lake

PLACE NAME	PRONUNCIATION	MAP	LOCATION
Encina	en-SEYE-noh	BKR	8 mil ↘ of Baker City
✉Endersby	EN-ders-bee	WAS	abt 3 mi ↖ of Dufer
Endicott Creek	ENDI-KAWT	COL	in S29 T6N R2W
Enid	EE-nid	LNE	abt 7 mi ↓ of Junction City.
Enola Hill	e-NOH-luh	CLK	↑ of the Zigzag Riv and ← of Devil Canyon
✉Enright	EN-reyet	TIL	siding on SPRR abt mid-way btwn Timber and Wheeler on Salmomberry Riv
✉Eola	ee-OH-luh	POK	on ← bank Willamette Riv abt 4 mi ↓ of Salem
✉Errol	EHR-ruhl	CLK	apparently nr MLT/CLK line on → side of Willamette Riv abt 6 mi ↙ from PDX
✉Erskineville	ER-skin	SHR	station on UPRR abt 4 mi ↙ of Moro. Hwy 97
Estabrook	ES-tah-brook	COO	abt 1 mi ↓ of Myrtle Point.
✉Estacada	es-tuh-KAY-duh	CLK	abt 14 miles ↘ of Oregon

City. Hwy 224. The Spanish pronunciation "es-ta-KAH-duh," a corruption of the original "Estacado," is not used by the locals. For the factors about this often argued pronunciation, see *Oregon Geographicv Names*

PLACE NAME	PRONUNCIATION	MAP	LOCATION
✉Estrup	es-TRUHP	LNE	nr Lake Cr, abt 10 mi ← of Junction City
✉Etelka	e-TEL-kah	COO	abt 10 mi ↓ of Myrtle Point
✉Etna	ET-nuh	POK	nr Baskett Slough a few miles ↑ of Rickreall
Euchre Creek	YOO-kuhr	CUR	crosses under Hwy 101 at Ophir
✉Euclid	YOO-kahlid	LIC	on Yachats Riv abt 6 mi ← of Fisher
✉Eula	YOO-luh	LNE	on SPRR abt 9 mi ↘ of Lowell
Ewauna (Lake)	*See* Lake Ewauna		
Ewe	YOO	JOE	nr Merlin. Hwy I-5
Ewing Young Hist Marker	YOO-ing	YAM	in Chehalem Valley

Postmark: ESTRUP FEB 21 1899 OREG.

Postmark: ENDERSLY SEP 25 1893 OREG.

PLACE NAME	PRONUNCIATION	MAP	LOCATION
⌂Faloma	fuh-LOH-muh	MLT	on ↓ bank Columbia Riv slightly → of Interstate Bridge (Hwy I-5) ↑ of PDX
Fandango Canyon	fan-DAN-goh	LKE	→ of Silver Lake
⌂Fangollano	fan-goh-LAH-noh	MAL	abt 8 mi ↗ of Cowley
Fanno	FAN-oh	WAH	abt 2 mi ↓ of Beaverton
Fanton	FEN-tahn	CLK	abt 10 mi ↘ of Estacada
Faraday Park	FER-a-dah	CLK	station at end of electric interurban RR at Cazadero and the Cazadero power plant on Clackamas Riv
Fargher	FAR-guhr	SHR	nr → end of Sherars Bridge
⌂Faubion	FAHB-ee-uhn	CLK	abt 1/2 mi ↘ of Zigzag. Hwy 26
Faught Creek	faw-t	CRK	↓ of Drake Butte
Fawcett Creek	FAW-set	TIL	↘ of Tillamook
Fellers	FE-lerz	MAR	RR station ↓ of Donald
Fennell Lake	FEN-uhl	LIN	↘ of Jefferson
Ferrelo (Cape)	*see:* Cape Ferello		
⌂Fife	FEYEF	CRK	"musical chairs" moving from place to place finally in ↘ area of cty. For details refer to Helbock - *See* bibliography
Finzer	FIN-zher	MAR	station on Oregon Electric Ry trolley line abt 5 mi ↙ of Salem
⌂Firholm	FUR-home	POK	abt 6 mi ↙ of Sheridan
⌂Flavel	flay-VEL	CLT	on Columbia Riv at Tansey Point abt 1 mi ↑ of Warrenton
Floras Lake	FLOH-ruhs	CUR	abt 3 mi ← of Langlois

separated from Pacific Ocean by narrow sand dune. On → shore is site of town of ⌂Lakeport. In WW-II, a major Coast Guard Beach Patrol here guarded against expected Japanese invation. See biblio for *Lakeport, Ghost Town of South Oregon Coast.*

PLACE NAME	PRONUNCIATION	MAP	LOCATION
Flounce Rock	FLOUGH-nse	JKS	abt 3 mi ↑ of Lost Cr Lake abt 6 mi ↙ of Prospect
Flournoy Valley	FLOHR-NOI	DGL	→ of Lookingglass
Fogerty Creek State Pk	FAWG-er-t	LIC	abt mid-way btwn Lincoln City and Newport. Hwy 101

Foley	FOH-lee	TIL	abt 8 mi ↓ of Nehalem
Fort Leland	fohrt LEE-luhnd	JOE	nr Grave Cr ↑ of Grants Pass in Sunny Valley. Hwy I-5

⚭Fort Stevens stee-vehns CLT on ↑ end of Clatsop Spit, abuts village of Hammond. Although established as a Civil War harbor defense fort, the only action seen was in World War II when on June 21, 1942, a Japanese Navy long-range submarine, *I-25*, shelled the fort. Refer to bibliography for *Silent Siege-III*

Fort Vannoy	van-NOI	JOE	Location of Rogue Community College campus abt 4 mi ← of Grants Pass. Hwy 199
Frazier	FRAYZ-er	LNE	station on SPRR abt 17 mi ← of Odell Lake
⚭Frieda	FREE-duh	WAS	abt 10 mi ↓ of Maupin at confluence of Deshutes Riv and Eagle Cr
⚭Friend	FREND	WAS	abt 14 mi ↙sw of Dufer
Frissell Point	friz-zel	LNE	↗ of McKenzie Bridge
Frizzell Ranch	fri-ZEL	WLR	on Upper Girds Cr
Froman	FROH-muhn	LIN	station on SPRR abt 2 mi ↘ of Albany
⚭Fruita	FROO-tuh	WAL	on Imnaha Riv nr Grouse abt 25 mi ↘ of Joseph

47

PLACE NAME	PRONUNCIATION	MAP	LOCATION
⌂Galena	ga-LEE-nuh	GRT	on Elk Cr abt 14 mi ↗ of Austin

⌂Galice	guhl-EESE	JOE	on Rogue Riv at confluence w/Galice Cr abt 15 mi ↖ of Grants Pass
⌂Garibaldi	gayr-i-BAWL-dee	TIL	on ↑ bank of Tillamook Bay abt 10 mi ↑ of Tillamook.
Garoutte Creek	garr-OT-ee	LNE	↓ of Black Butte
Garrigus Creek	garr-e-gus	WAH	nr Manning
Gasco	GAS-koh	MLT	station on RR on ← bank of Willamette Riv abt 1 mi ↑ of St. Johns
⌂Gaston	GAS-tuhn	WAH	abt 6 mi ↓ of Forest Grove
Gauldy (Mountain)	gawl-dee	TIL	↓ of Hebo. Elev. 2,227 ft. *See* HEBO TOPO
⌂Gaylord	GAY-lohrd	COO	abt mid-way btwn Myrtle Point and Powers abt 9 mi ↑ of Powers
⌂Gazley	gayz-lee	DGL	↑ of So. Umpqua Riv and abt 5 mi ↗ of Canyonville
Gearhart Mountain	GEER-hahrt	LKE	elev. 8,364 ft. abt 11 mi ↗ of Bly (Klamath County) in Fremont Nat'l Forest. A Japanese balloon bomb exploded here in World War II killing 5 children and an adult who were on a picnic. These are the only civilian deaths on continental USA in WWII as a result of direct Japanee action. Refer to biblio for *Silent Siege III*. Refer to illustrations under <u>Bly</u> on page 25. *See* CAMPBRLL RIVER TOPO
Geer	GEER	MAR	RR station → of Salem
Geisel Monument	GI-zehl	CUR	abt 7 mi ↑ of Gold Beach.
⌂Geiser	g-EYE-ser	BKR	abt 9 mi ↙ of Sumpter
⌂Geneva	juh-NEE-vuh	JEF	abt 5 mi ↙ of Grandview
Gerlinger	GER-ling-er	POK	RR crossing abt 1 mi ↓ of Derry

PLACE NAME	PRONUNCIATION	MAP	LOCATION
Gervais	JER-vuhs	MAR	abt 3 mi ⬋ of Woodburn
Gesner	GES-ner	MAR	RR station → of Salem
Gilchrist	GIL-krist	KLA	1 mi ↑ of Crescent abt 45 mi ↓ of Bend. Hwy 97
Gilkey	GIL-kee	LIN	abt 12 mi ↑ of Lebanon
Gillis	GIL-is	MLT	abt 3 mi → of Gresham
Glenada	glen-AY -duh	LNE	on ↓ bank of Siuslaw Riv opposite Florence
Glencoe	GLEN-koh	WAH	a district in North Plains abt 5 mi ↑ of Hillsboro
Glencullen	glen-KUHL-en	MLT	district in ⬋ part of PDX
Glendale	GLEN-dayl	DGL	in Cow Cr abt 15 mi ⬋ of Canyonville

Gleneden Beach	glen-EED-uhn	LIN	abt 4 miles ↓ of Lincoln City. Hwy 101
Glentena	glen-TEN-uh	LNE	abt 3 mi ↘ of Meadow
Glisan Glacier	GLEE-san	HDR	on ↗ slope of Mount Hood
Goble	gough-bul	COL	on Columbia Riv abt 7 mi ↓ of Rainier. Hwy 30
Goltra	GAHL-truh	LIN	RR station btwn Albany and Lebanon
Gooch	GOOCH	LIN	RR station abt 2 mi ← of Mill City
Goshen	GOHS-un	LNE	abt 6mi ↘ of Eugene. Hwy I-

49

PLACE NAME	PRONUNCIATION	MAP	LOCATION
⌂Goshen	GOHS-un	LNE	abt 6mi ↘ of Eugene. Hwy I-5
Gourlay Creek	gerl-ee	COL	tributary of So. Scappoose Cr. *See* DIXIE MOUNTAIN TOPO
⌂Government Camp	guv-ehrn-ment	CLK	elev. 3,880 ft. On original Barlow Rd, now Hwy 26 abt 10 mi → of Rhodendron
Grabenhorst Corners	GRAY-buhn-horst	MAR	abt 4 mi ↓ of Salem. Hwy 99E
Graeme	GRAY-em	CLK	abt 2 mi ← of Wilsonville
Grande Ronde	grand-rownd	POK/YAM	since 1924 the postoffice has been in Polk County. Hwy 18
⌂Granite	gra-nit	GRT	at confluence of Bull Run and Granite crs ↗ of Sumpter

PLACE NAME	PRONUNCIATION	MAP	LOCATION
Greiner Canyon	GREYE-nor	GIL	↓ of Condon
⌂Gresham	GRESH-am	MLT	abt 14 mi → of PDX. Hwy I-84
Gribble Prairie	grib-ul	CLK	abt 3 mi ↓ of Canby
Grouslous Mountain	grow-sluhs	CUR	on SIXES TOPO
Guano Lake	GWA-noh	LKE	in T39S, R27E
Gumboot Creek	GUHM-boot	WAL	in ↙ part of cty
Gumjuwac Saddle	guhm-joo-wak	HDR	1 mi ↙ of Lookout Mtn
Gunaldo Falls	guhn-AWL-doh	YAM	on Sourgrass Cr btwn Hebo and Grand Ronde Yambill County 1 mi ← of Dolph
⌂Gurdane	jer-DAYN	UMT	abt mid-way btwn Vinson and Albee abt 14 miles ↖ of Uktah
⌂Gwendolen	gwendoh-luhn	GIL	abt 9 mi ↑ of Condon
⌂Gypsum	gyp-suhm	BKR	on ← bank of Snake Riv abt 5 mi ↗ of Huntington. Hwy I-84

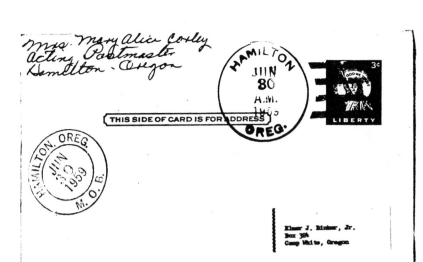

PLACE NAME	PRONUNCIATION	MAP	LOCATION
Haas Ridge	HA-ss	WAL	↗ area of cty ← of Lightening Cr. *See* SLEEPY RIDGE TOPO
Haddon	had-duhn	TIL	abt 17 mi ↑ of Tillamook
Hadleyville	HAD-le-vil	LNE	abt 4 mi ↘ of Crow on Coyote Cr
Haig	HAYG	MLT	district in ↘ PDX
Haines	HAYNS	BKR	30 mi ↖ Baker City. Hwy 30
Hager	hay-ger	KLM	abt 3 mi ↘ of Klamath Falls
Hager Mountain	HAY-ger	LKE	elev. 7,185 ft. abt 10 mi ↓ of Silver Lake *See* HAGER MT TOPO
Haley	hay-lee	CLK	station on RR 1 mi ↖ of Boring
Halsey	HAWL-see	LIN	17 mi ↓ of Albany. Hwy 99E
Hamilton	HAM-el-tun	GRT	abt 10 mi ⟲ of Monument abt mid-way between Monument and Long Creek on Deer Cr
Hammersley	HAM-merz-lee	JOE	at a mine ↗ of Grants Pass where a PO was approved but probably never operated
Harmony	HAHR-moh-nee	CLK	abt 2 mi → of Milwaukie
Harriman	hair-i-man	HAR	on ↗ bank og Malheur Lk abt 3 mi w of Crane
Hauser	HOW-zer	COO	station on SPRR abt 7 mi ↑ of North Bend

51

The highway sign (left) and the motel sign are on the east side of Hwy 101 within a couple hundred feet of each other about 4 miles north of Florence.
—Photo by Bert Webber - Oct. 1994

PLACE NAME	PRONUNCIATION	MAP	LOCATION
Havana	HAV-VAN-nuh	UMT	abt 7 mi ↖ of Pendleton
Hawley Creek	HAW-lee	BEN	nr Alpine ← of Monroe
Hayden Island	HAY-duhn	MLT	within Columbia Riv btwn PDX and Vancouver, Wash.
Hazelau	HAYZ-uh-law	MAR	station on Oregon Electric Ry abt 2 mi ↘ of Salem
Hazelia	hayz-cl-EE-uh	CLK	abt 4 mi → of Tualatin
⌂Hebo	HEE-boh	TIL	3 mi ↗ of Cloverdale at Hwys 22/101
⌂Heceta	he-SEE-tuh	LNE	abt 4 mi ↑ of Florence.

Hwy 101. Locals say it "heck-ka-tuh" in the face of the Spanish "Ay-thay-tah" which is at the root correct, having been named for Spanish explorer Bruno Heceta.

PLACE NAME	PRONUNCIATION	MAP	LOCATION
Hehe Butte	hee-hee	WAS	elev. 3,090 ft. on Warm Springs Ind. Reser. *See* HEHE BUTTE TOPO
⌂Heisler	HEYE-sler	JEF	on Hay Cr ↗ of Madras
⌂Helix	hee-liks	UMT	abt 15 mi ↗ of Pendleton on Burlington Northern RR
⌂Helloff	hel-ahf	TIL	abt 10 mi ↗ of Wheeler
Helvetia	hel-VEE-she-ah	WAH	on North Plains
⌂Hembree	HEM-bree	TIL	abt 1mi → of Sand Lake on Sand Cr
⌂Hemlock	HEM-LAWK	TIL	abt 4 mi ↑ of Beaver.
⌂Hemstad	hem-STAD	DES	abt 15 mi ↙ of Brothers
Henrici	hen-REE-see	CLK	abt 8 mim ↗ of Mulino
⌂Hereford	HER-fohrd	BKR	abt 11 mi → of Unity Lake

⌂Hershal	her-shuhl	BKR	abt 6 mi ↘ of McEwan
Hilgard Jct State Park	HIL-gahrd	UNN	abt 8 mi ↖ of LaGrande
Hindman	HEYE-nd-man	BKR	abt 14 mi ↘ of Baker
Hiteon	HIT-ee-on	WAH	abt 4 mi ↓ of Beaverton
Hiyu Mountain	HEYE-yoo	CLK	elev. 4,654 ft. ↓ of Bull Run Lake. *See* BULL RUN TOPO
⌂Hoaglin	HOHG-lin	DGL	on N.Umpqua Riv abt 4 mi ↗ of Glide
⌂Hobsonville	HAHB-suhn-vil	TIL	on Miami Cove abt 3 mi ↓ of Garibaldi and abt 8 mi ↑ of Tillamook
⌂Hoevet	HOH-vett	TIL	was abt 1 mi ← of town at a lumber

PLACE NAME	PRONUNCIATION	MAP	LOCATION

 Holbrook — hohl-bru-k — MLT site on ← bank Multnomah Channel across from Sauvie Isl

 Holladay — HAHL-uh-day — CLT site of postoffice and terminal station at end-of-track of Astoria & Columbia River Railroad abt 1 mi ↓ of downtown Seaside on the Necanicum Riv. It was named for Ben Holladay famous for Hollday's Stage Coach lines and an Oregon railroad pioneer. The postoffice lasted about 10 months —June 1890 - Apr 1891. During WW-II, the railroad hauled munitions to Fort Stevens and freight cars full of Pres-To-Logs to heat the tents at Camp Clatsop, as well as passengers through to Seaside, until about 1950. The rails are now gone.

 Holley — HAH-lee — LIN ↑ of Calapooya Riv abt 4 mi ↙ of Sweet Home

Homly — HOHM-lee — UMT station on UPRR → of Cayuse, abt 13 mi → of Pendleton

Hooskanaden — HOOS-kah-nahd-en — CUR a cr nw of Carpenterville. *See* CARPENTERVILLE TOPO

Hopmere — HAHP-meer — MAR station on Oregon Electric Ry abt 9 mi → of Salem

Hoquarten Slough — hoh-kwohr-tuhn — TIL a part of Tillamook Bay immediately in front of city of Tillamook

Horeb (Mountain) — hohr-eb — MAR is 4,212 ft. elev abt 8 mi ↗ of Mill City. *See* ELKHORN TOPO

 Hoskins — HAHS-kins — BEN on Luckiamute Riv abt 3 mi ↙ of Kings Valley

Howe — HOW — YAM abt 3 mi ↓ of Carlton

 Huber — HYOO-ber — WAH postoffice and station abt 6 mi ← of Beaverton

Hughey Creek — hyoo-ee — TIL abt 9 mi ↓ of Corvallis

Hulbert Lake — huhl-bert — LNE 4 mi ← of Harrisburg

 Hullt — huhl-t — MAR abt 12 mi ↘ of Silverton nr Silver Creek Falls

PLACE NAME	PRONUNCIATION	MAP	LOCATION
Ibex	EYE-bex	CRK	abt 8 mi ↗ of Hampton
Ida	EYE-duh	LNE	abt 17 mi ↓ of Cottage Grove on Coast Fork Willamette Riv.
Idanha	eye-DAN-uh	MAR	on ↑ bank Santiam Riv abt 4 mi → of Detroit

Idaville	EYE-duh-vil	TIL	abt 3 mi ↑ of Tillamook
Idleyld Park	EYE-duh-weyeld	DGL	on N.Umpqua Riv ↗ of Rock Cr abt 1 mi → of present Idleyld Park and 3 mi ↗ of Glide. Hwy 138
Idol	EYE-dul	HAR	site at head of Trout Cr abt 10 mi ↑ of Harney
Igo	igg-ough	GIL	elev. 3,125 ft. abt 7 mi ↗ of Condon. See IGO BUTTE TOPO
Ikt Butte	ikt	DES	See LAVA CAST FOREST TOPO
Ila	EYE-lah	DGL	abt 3 mi ↙ of London nr Lane Cty line.
Illahe	IL-uh-hee	CUR	6 mi upstream from Agnes on the Rogue Riv.

Imbler	IM-bler	UNN	8 mi ↓ of Elgin
Imnaha	im-NAH-hah	WAL	abt 30 twisting mi ↗ of Joseph, 8 air-miles ↘ of Zumwalt
Inavale	in-uh-vayl	BEN	3 mi ↙ of Corvallis

55

PLACE NAME	PRONUNCIATION	MAP	LOCATION
Indigo Creek	IN-dee-goh	CUR LKE LNE	There are 3 Indigo creeks listed in *Oregon Geographic Names System*
⌂Ingles	IN-guls	WAH	abt 2 mi ↑ of Cornelius on Diary Cr
⌂Inglis	IN-guhls	COL	a RR station and postoffice abt mid-way btwn Clatskanie and Quincy aby 2 mi ↘ of Quincy
⌂Ione	EYE-ohn	MOR	abt 9 mi ↖ of Lexington Hwy 74
Ipsoot Butte	ip-soot	KLM	elev. 5,275 ft. in ↗ corner of cty . *See* SPRING BUTTE TOPO
⌂Irrigon	EAR-uh-guhn	MOR	On Columbia Riv 7 mi ← of Umatilla. Hwy 730
Isadore Ranch	iz-ah-DOHR	CRK	in Rabbit Valley. elev. 3,880 ft. *See* RABBIT VALLEY TOPO
⌂Isolate	EYE-soh-layt	DGL	in an isolated mountain area abt 12 mi ↗ of Canyonville
Isthmus Slough	IS-muhs	COO	1 mi ↓ of Coos Bay
⌂Ivison	EYE-vi-suhn	LNE	site of PO on Wildcat Cr abt 9 mi → of Walton
⌂Izee	EYE-zee	GRT	on So.Fork John Day Riv

18 mi ↙ of Logdell on a picturesque twisty county road that runs ← from Hwy 395 ↓ of Canyon City

PLACE NAME	PRONUNCIATION	MAP	LOCATION
Jakey Ridge	Jay-kee	WAL	abt 8 mi ↑ of Hat Point. *See* SLEEPY RIDGE TOPO
Jalland Creek	jal-AND	HDR	*See* FLAG POINT TOPO
🏤Jamieson	JAY-mi-suhn	MAL	8 mi ↖ of Keating
🏤Jantzen Beach	jan-sen	MLT	on Hayden Isl in Columbia Riv ↑ of PDX. Hwy I-5
Jarboe Meadow	JAHR-boh	UNN	abt 15 mi ↑ of Elgin
Jaussaud Corral	JAW-suhd	WAL	abt 17 mi ↗ of Tollgate. *See also* FRY MEADOW TOPO
Jaynes Ridge	jayns	WAL	in ↘ area of cty
🏤Jennyopolis	je-nee-AH-pawl-is	BEN	site on Muddy Cr abt 8 mi ↓ of Corvallis
Joler	joh-ler	LNE	*See* CLAY CREEK TOPO
🏤Joppa	jaw-puh	WAH	a postoffice (1874-1876) presumed to have been abt 8 mi ↖of Forest Grove but records are missing or indefinite
🏤Juniper	JOON-i-per	UMT	abt 6 mi ↖ of Helix. There were two postoffices "Juniper" — one each in Umatilla and Lake counties
🏤Juntura	juhn-ter-uh	MAL	on Malheur Riv abt midway btwn Vale and Burns. Hwy 20

PLACE NAME	PRONUNCIATION	MAP	LOCATION
Kah-Nee-Ta	kah-NEE-tuh	WAS	↑of Warm Springs
Kapka Butte	KAAP-ka	DES	elev. 6,170 ft. nr Tumalo Mt. *See* WANOGA BUTTE TOPO
Kaleetan Butte	KAL-ee-tan	DES	elev. 6,800 ft. SOUTH SISTER TOPO
⌂Kamela	KA-mel-lah	UNN	on RR abt 6 mi ↓ of Meacham close to UMT/UNN line
⌂Kaskela	kas-KE-lah	WAS	once a RR station on → side of Deschutes Riv abt 12 mi ↑ of Gateway
Katsuk Butte	KAT-suk	DES	elev. 6,165 ft. *See* SOUTH SISTER TOPO (Also a Katsuk Butte in Lane Cty)
Kawak Butte	KUH-wak	DES	elev. 7,370 ft. *See* LAVA CAST FOREST TOPO
⌂Keasey	KEE-zer	COL	site of postoffice when

opened was in farm house abt 4 mi → of COL/CLT line abt 8 miles ← of Vernonia. After it closed, the owner of East Side Logging Co. built a new postoffice at a large RR switch yard almost on the line but still in COL cty, where it would serve his needs, then he convinced the gov't to occupy and run it. *See* biblio for *Swivel-Chair Logger.* When author visited site in early 1980's, area was overgrown with weeds there being no trace of buildings or any of the large RR switchyard.

PLACE NAME	PRONUNCIATION	MAP	LOCATION
⌂Keizer	keye-zer	MAR	on 4 bank of Willmette Riv., abutts → edge of Salem. Hwy 219 and I-5. *see also* Kizer, Kyser
⌂Kelleher	KEL-eh-her	DGL	← of Yoncalla on Billy Cr
⌂Keno	KEE-noh	KLM	on ↓ bank of Klamath Riv abt 12 mi ↙ of Klamath Falls
Ketchketch Butte	KECH-KECH	DES	elev. 5,395 ft. ↙ of Crane Prairie. See CRANE PRAIRIE TOPO
Kiechle Arm	kee-chel	LNE	arm or bay of Siltcoos Lake
Kiger Island	KEYE-ger	BEN	in Willamette Riv ↘ of Corvallis

PLACE NAME	PRONUNCIATION	MAP	LOCATION

⌐Kilchis   KIL-chis   TIL   on → shore of Tillamook Bay nr mouth of Kilchis Riv abt 7 mi ↖ of Tillamook. Hwy 101

Killamacue Creek   KIL-uh-muh-kyoo   BKR   drains Killamocue Lake

Kimball Hill   KIM-buhl   CUR   abt mi 4 → of the Pacific Ocean near the → bank of the Rogue Riv

Kincheloe Point   KINCH-loh   TIL   the ↑ point of Tillamook Spit, also called Bayocean Spit for the town that was developed there. *See* bibliography for *Bayocean, The Oregon Town That Fell Into The Sea*

Kinzel Creek   KIN-sel   CLK   ↓of Rhododendron

⌐Kinzua   KIN-zoo   WLR   abt 10 mi → of Fossil

KINZUA, OR
MAY
30
PM
1973
97849

Kishwalks   KISH-WAWKS   WAS   on Warm Springs Indian Reser

Kittredge Lake   KIT-rej   MLT   small overflow lake on ← bank of Willamette Riv → of Oilton (not Kittredge)

Kiwa Butte   KEYE-wuh   DES   elev. 5,900 ft. ↙ of Bend. *See* WANOGA BUTTE TOPO

Kiwanda Cape   *See* Cape Kiwanda

Kizer   KEYE-zer   LNE   abt 5 mi → of Cottage Grove. *See also* Keizer; Kyser

Klak Butte   KLAK   DES   elev. 4,842 ft. ↙ of Bend. *See* PISTOL TOPO

Klaskanine River   KLAS-kuh-neyen   CLT   different than Clatskanai River in Columbia Cty. *See* OLNEY TOPO

Klawhop Butte   KLAW-hawp   DES   elev. 5,512 ft. *See* LAVA BUTTE TOPO

Klickitat Mountain   KLIK-i-tat   LNE   elev. 2.307 ft. *See* CUMMINS PEAK TOPO

Kloan   KLOHN   WAS   site of RR station nr ↑ end of Deschutes Riv canyon abt 12 mi ↘ of The Dalles

59

PLACE NAME	PRONUNCIATION	MAP	LOCATION
☎Klondike	KLAWN-deyek	SHR	station on RR; today's village nearly a ghost town abt 6 mi → of Wasco
Kloochman Creek	KLOOCH-muhn	CRK	flows ↓ from Maury Mountains
Klovdahl Bay	KLUHV-dahl	LNE	bay on Waldo Lake
☎Klumb	KLUHM	MAR	abt 3 mi ↑ of Mehama
☎Knappa	NA-puh	CLT	abt 17 mi → of Astoria. Hwy 30
Knox Butte	NAWX	LIN	elev. 540 ft. abt 6 mi → of Albany. *See* ALBANY TOPO
Kokostick Butte	KOH-koh-stik	DES	elev. 6,740 ft. nr Devils Lake. *See* SOUTH SISTER TOPO
Koosah Mountain	KOO-sah	LIN	elev. 6,520 ft. on McKenzie Riv. *See* SOUTH SISTER TOPO
Kotan	KOUGH-tayne	KLM	station on SPRR ↘ of Odell Lake
☎Kreigh	CRY	LKE	Site of PO in Yokum Valley abt 1 mi ↑ of California line
☎Kronenberg	KROHN-nen-berg	MLT	PO site was at corner of SE 162nd St and Powell Blvd. earlier occupied by Meadowland Dairy in PDX
Krumbo Mountian	KRUHM-boh	HAR	*See* KROMBO RIDGE TOPO
Kuamaksi Butte	kwahm-AH-skee	DES	elev. 5,265 ft. ↙ of Bend. *See* WAGONA BUTTE TOPO
☎Kubli	KOO-blee	JKS	on Caris Cr 2 mi ↑ of Provolt
Kweo Butte	KWAY-ough	DES	elev. 6,873 ft. in Newberry National Volcanic Monument. *See* biblio for **Newberry National Volcanic Monument** and EAST LAKE TOPO
Kwinnum Butte	kwin-nuhm	DES	elev. 6,232 ft. *See* FUZZTAIL BUTTE TOPO
Kwolh Butte	kloh	DES	elev. 7,358 ft. abt 2 mi ↓ of Bachelor Butte., *See* BACHELOR BUTTE TOPO
Kyser	KEYE-zer	COL	abt 2 mi ↓ of Delena on Lost Cr. *See also* Keiser and Kizer

60

PLACE NAME	PRONUNCIATION	MAP	LOCATION
Labish	la-BISH	MAR	6 mi ↑ of Salem
Lackemute	laq-uh-moot	POK	variation on Luckiamute.

This "musical chairs" PO moved around btwn 1851-1874. Helbock (which see) says no printed postmarks, only manuscript (pen & ink) exist. *See also Oregon Geographic Names*

Lacomb	luh-kohm	LINN	9 mi ↗ of Salem
Lafayette	lay-fay-ET	YAM	abt 6 mi ↗ of McMinnville
LaGrande	luh-GRAND	UNN	abt mid-way btwn Pendleton and Baker City on Hwy I-84
Laidlaw Butte	layd-law	DES	elev. 3,497 ft. 1 mi ← of Tumalo. *See* TUMALO TOPO
Lake Chetlo	chet-loh	LNE	↖ of Waldo Lake
Lake Ewauna	ee-WAW-nuh	KLM	an elbow in Klamath Lake
Lake Labish	luh-BISH	MAR	marsh area → of Brooks
Lake Lytle	leye-TELL	TIL	abt 3 mi ↑ of Bar View. Hwy 101
Lakeport	*See* Floras Lake		
Lamberson Butte	LAM-ber-suhn	HDR	elev. 6,633 ft. → of Mt Hood *See* MOUNT HOOD SOUTH TOPO
Lamonta	la-MON-TUH	CRK	abt 9 mi ↘ of Culver
La Mu	luh-MOO	HAR	site was → of Malheur Lake near village of Crane. Hwy 78
Langell's Valley	LAN-juhl	KLM	site of postoffice abt 10 mi ↘ of Bonanza
Langlois	LANG-lois	CUR	abt 14 mi ↓ of Bandon.
Lapine	luh-PEYEN	DES	30 mi ↓ of Bend. Hwy 97

at entrance to Newberry National Volcano Monument. *See* biblio for *Newberry National Volcanic Monument.*

Laraut	lah-ROH	DGL	abt 5 mi ← of Winchester
Latham	LAY-thuhm	LNE	2 mi ↓ of Cottage Grove

PLACE NAME	PRONUNCIATION	MAP	LOCATION
🏚Latourell Falls	lat-er-EL	MLT	postoffice on UPRR nr the waterfall 2 miles → of Troutdale
🏚Laurel	LAW-ruhl	WAH	abt 7 mi ↓ of Hillsboro
Laverty Lakes	LA-ver-tee	WAL	See NORTH MINAM MEADOWS TOPO
Lavacicle Cave	LAH-vah-cikle	DEL	abt 35 mi ↘ of Bend. See PILOT BUTTE TOPO
Lavadoure Creek	LAH-vah-dohr	DGL	abt 5 mi above Days Creek
🏚Lawen	LAWN	HAR	17 mi ↘ of Burns. Hwy 78
Lazarus Island	laz-uh-ruhs	TIL	in Nehalem River opposite Wheeler
🏚Lebanon	LEB-uh-nuhn	LIN	12 mi ↘ of Albany
Le Conte Crater	le-KAHNT	DES/LNE	on summit of Cascade mts ↓ of South Sister. See SOUTH SISTER TOPO
Lefevre Prairie	la-fee-ver	G-3	abt 19 mi ↙ of Harriman
🏚Lehman	LAY-men	UMT	elev. 4,430 ft. at Lehman

Springs. A health resort operated here for many years, now known as Lehman Hot Springs Rec. Site abt 13 mi → of Ukiah. Hwy 244. See LEHMAN SPRINGS TOPO.

🏚Leland	LEE-luhnd	JOE	6 mi ↙ of Wolf Creek. Hwy I-5
Leloo Lake	lee-loo	DGL	reservoir on N. Umpqua Riv
🏚Lemati	la-MAT-e	LNE	station on Oregon & Central RR on → side of Little Coast Fork Riv across from Cottage Grove
Lemish Butte	lee-mish	DES	← of Crane Prairie
🏚Leneve	LEN-EV	COO	postoffice site 4 mi ↑ of Riverton
Lenox	len-awx	WAH	abt 1 mi ↓of Helvetia / 4 mi ↙ of Glencoe
🏚Lents	LENTS	MLT	district in ↘ PDX

PLACE NAME	PRONUNCIATION	MAP	LOCATION
🖂Liberal	LI-ber-ahl	CLK	abt 3 mi ↑ of Molalla
🖂Linkville	linck-ville	KLM	original name for Klamath Falls. Hwy 97

Linnemann	LIN-ne-mun	MNL	station on Portland Traction (street car) Co. line abt 2 mi ← of Gresham
Linneus	LIN-e-us	LNE	abt 8 mi ↗ of Florence on Siuslaw Riv
Linney Butte	lin-nee	CLK	elev. 4,800 ft. *See* HIGH ROCK TOPO
🖂Linslaw	LINS-slau	LNE	on Siuslaw Riv abt 8 mi ↙ of Walton
🖂Llano	LAN-o	MAL	abt 10 mi ↖ of Vale nr

confluence of Cottonwood and Bully Crs. The name is Spanish but local contemoraries use the hard pronunciation as shown

🖂Linnton	LIN-ton	MLT	on ← bank of Willamette Riv ↖ of St Johns both now districts of PDX
Little Wocus Bay	WOH-kuhs	KLM	↓ of Klamath Marsh
🖂Llano	lah-noh	MAL	abt 10 mi ↖ of Vale
Llao Rock	lay-oh	KLM	elev. 8,046 ft. on ↗ rim of Crater Lake.
🖂Llewellyn	luh-WEL-in	LNE	abt 5 mi ↗ of Crow
Locada	loh-KOH-duh	COL	station on SP&S RR ↗ of Clatskanie
🖂Logan	lo-gan	CLK	abt 5 mi ↑ of Viola and abt 10 mi → of Oregon City
Lolah Butte	loh-lah	DES	elev. 5,310 ft. ↗ of Crane Prairie. *See* ROUND MOUNTAIN TOPO

63

PLACE NAME	PRONUNCIATION	MAP	LOCATION
Lolo Pass	LOH-loh	HDR	at summit of Cascade mts abt 2 mi ↓ of Bull Run Lake. *See* BULL RUN LAKE TOPO
✉Lonsomehurst	LON-suhm-hurst	HAR	abt 20 mi ↑ of Burns on Hardesty Ranch
✉Lorane	la-rayne	LNE	abt 13 mi ← of Cottage Grove
✉Lorella	loh-REL-luh	KLM	abt 9 miles ↘ of Bonanza
✉Lostine	LAWS-teen	WAL	abt 9 mi ↖ of Enterprise on Lostine Riv.
Lousignont Lake	LOO-sig-nahnt	WAH	site about 5 mi ↖ of Forest Grove - lake mostly drained
Luckiamute	LUK-ee-meoot	POK	the Lackemute post office was apparently on or nr the Luckiamute Riv a liitle ← of Hwy 99W in ↓ end of cty. *See* Helbock in biblio
✉Luda	loo-dah	COO	on E.Fork Coquille River 4 mi → of Gravel Ford
Lukens Creek	loo-kuhns	CLK	*See* SOOSAP PEAK TOPO
Lumrum Butte	luhm-ruhm	DES	elev. 5,295 ft. ↗ of Craine Prairie . *See* ROUND MOUNTAIN TOPO
Lun	luhn	UNN	abt 12 mi ↓ of Union
Luse	loos	MAL	site of RR station btwn Ontario and Vale abt 10 mi → of Vale. Hwys 20/26
Lytle (Lake)	*See* Lake Lytel		

PLACE NAME	PRONUNCIATION	MAP	LOCATION
Macleay	muh-KLAY	MAR	abt 10 mi → of Salem

Mahan   may-han   WAH   1 mi ↑ of Hillsboro

Maidu Lake   may-dyoo   DGL   elev. 5,980 ft.
See BURN BUTTE TOPO

Madras   MAD-ruhs   JEF   abt 44 mi ↑ of Bend. Hwy 97

Malheur   mal-HYOO-er   MAL   name for a cty and PO the
PO site abt 7 mi ↓ of Bridgeport

Malin   muh-LIN   KLM   abt 8 mi → of Merrill. Hwy 39

Mallett   MAL-let   MAL   abt 6 mi → of Vale

Manseneta   man-zen-et-ah   JKS   (location undetermined)

Manzanita   MAN-zuh-NEE-tuh   TIL   abt 2 mi ← of Nehalem.

Marcola   mahr-COH-luh   LNE   abt 18 mi ↗ of Springfield

Marial   MAHR-ree-ahl   CUR   in the wild section of the
Rogue River abt 16 mi → of Illahee

Marquam   M-AHR-kuhm   CLK   abt 4 mi ↘ of Monitor

Marylhurst   MEHR-il-herst   CLK   on the grounds of Marylhurst
College 1 mi south of Lake Oswego. Hwy 43

Matheny Creek   ma-THIN-ee   COO   west of Myrtle Point.
See MYRTLE POINT TOPO

Matoles   ma-tohls   JEF   on Lake Cr abt 1 mi ↓ of
Camp Sherman

Matthieu Lakes   MATH-yoo   DES   *See* NORTH SISTER TOPO

Maud   mawd   JEF   nr Pony Butte abt 10 mi ←
of Ashwood. *See* WILLOWDALE TOPO

Maupin   MAWP-in   WAS   in a steep valley at
confluence of Deschutes Riv and Bakeoven Cr. Hwy 197

65

PLACE NAME	PRONUNCIATION	MAP	LOCATION
Maury Mountains	MOW-ree	CRK	*See* MULE DEER RANGE TOPO. *See also* Mowry
✉Mayger	MAY-gur	COL	on Columbia Riv abt 7 mi ↗ of Clatskanie
✉McDermitt	mak-DER-mit	MAL	elev. 4,111 ft. on Nevada border. PO started in Nevada, moved to Oregon, then moved back in 1908. Hwy 95. *See* MCDERMITT (NV) TOPO
✉McEwen	muhk-YOO-uhn	BKR	on Powder Riv abt 6 mi → of Sumpter. Hwy 7
✉McGlynn	ma-gulinn	LNE	on SPRR at Penn Station on Wildcat Cr. abt 4 mi → of Walton
McKendree	muh-KEN-dree	KLM	abt 13 mi ↘ of Klamath Falls. Hwy 39
✉McMinnville	muhk-MIN-vil	YAM	Hwy 18/99W
✉McNary	muhk-NE-ree	UMT	3 mi → of Umatilla. Hwy 730
✉Mealey	MAY-lee	LIN	abt 7 mi ↘ of Foster
✉Mears (Cape)	*See* Cape Meares		
✉Mecca	me-kuh	JEF	on → bank Deschutes Riv on old hwy
✉Medford	MED-fuhrd	JKS	on Bear Cr 4 mi ↓ of Central Point. Hwy I-5
✉Mehama	muh-HAY-muh	MAR	on N.Santiam Riv abt 9 mi → of Stayton
✉Melrose	MEL-rohz	DGL	abt 6 mi ← of Roseburg
Memaloose Island	MEM-ah-loos	WAS	btwn The Dalles and Mosier opposite the safety rest area on Hwy I-84. *See* LYLE (WA) TOPO
Menefee	MEN-e-fee	CLK	abt 1 mi ↓ of Milwaukie
Meno	men-oh		*See* Menominee
✉Menominee	men-AH-mun-nee	HDR	on Columbia Riv, PO at station on UPRR (old OWR&N) abt 4 mi w of Hood River. After PO closed (1913), name changed to Meno

66

PLACE NAME	PRONUNCIATION	MAP	LOCATION
Merganser	mer-GAN-zer	KLM	abt 2 mi ↓ of Klamath Falls
Meridian	mer-ID-ee-uhn	MAR	abt 2 mi ↓ of Monitor
Merlin	MUHR-lin	JOE	7 mi ↖ of Grants Pass. Hwy I-5
Merrill	MER-uhl	KLM	10 miles ← of Malin
Mesa Creek	may-suh	LNE	↓ of Three Sisters. *See* SOUTH SISTER TOPO
Metolius	muh-TOH-lee-uhs	JEF	station on old Oregon Trunk RR abt 6 mi ↓ of Madras
Metzger	MET-zguhr	WAH	abt 2 mi ← and 1 mi ↓ of Multnomah, later moved to Hwy 217 and Locust Dr.
Meva	MEE-vuh	KLM	abt 4 mi ↗ of Chiloquin
Mikkalo	mick-ahl-oh	GIL	station abt 5 mi ↑ of Clem on the CHINA, PACIFIC, CONDON, KINUZA & SOUTHERN RR
Millican	MIL-i-kuhn	DES	abt 22 mi ↗ of Bend and abt 15 mi ← of Brothers. Hwy 20
Millicoma River	mil-i-KOH-muh	COO	abt 8 mi ↗ of Coos Bay. *See* ALLEGANY TOPO
Milo	MEYE-loh	DGL	abt mid-way btwn Days Creek and Tiller
Minam	Minn-em	WAL	at confluence of Minam and Wallowa Rivs abt 14 mi ↗ of Elgin. Hwy 82
Minerva	min-ER-vuli	LNE	on N.Fork of Siuslaw Riv abt 10 mi ↗ of Mapleton
Minto	MIN-toh	MAR	on N.Santiam Riv abt 5 mi → of Mill City

PLACE NAME	PRONUNCIATION	MAP	LOCATION

Mishawaka — mish-aw-WAW-kah — CLT — abt 2 mi → of Elsie

Missouri Flat — mi-ZUHR-ee (also pron: mi-ZUR-uh) — BKR — elev. 3,370 ft. *See* BAKER TOPO (There is a <u>Missouri Flat</u> in Josephine Cty)

Modoc Point — MOH-dahk — KLM — on → side of Klamath Lake abt 15 mi ↑ of Klamath Falls. Hwy 97. The PO was abt 8 mi ↓ of Chiloquin in SPRR station

Mofat — MA-faht — WAH — station on Oregon Electric Ry on → side of Hillsboro

Mohawk — MOH-haw-k — LNE — abt 7 mi ↗ of Springfield on Mohawk Riv

Mohler — MOH-ler — TIL — abt 2 mi → of Nehalem

Mokst Butte — MAWKST — DES — elev. 6,162 ft. *See* LAVA CAST FOREST TOPO

Molalla — MOH-la-luh — CLK — abt 8 mi → of Woodburn. Hwys junction 211/213

Monitor — MAHN-i-ter — MAR — abt 3 mi ↗ of Mt. Angel

Monkland — mun-kland — SHR — abt 6 mi → of Moro

Monmouth — MAHN-muhth — POK — abt 12 mi ↙ of Salem

Montague — MAHN-tuh-goo — GIL — abt 9 mi ↘ of Arlington where the Oregon Trail crossed Eightmile Canyon abt 3 mi → of Shutler

Monument — MOHN-yoo-mehnt — GRT — abt 13 mi → of Kimberly on N.Fork John Day Riv abt mid-way btwn Hamilton and Kimberly

JOSEPH PUTNAM
BREEDER OF
rade Percheron Horses
AND
POLAND CHINA HOGS
ment, Grant Co.,   Oregon

68

PLACE NAME	PRONUNCIATION	MAP	LOCATION
⌖Moorhouse	MOOER-howze	UMT	abt 5 mi → of Echo
Moosmoos Creek	moos-moos	CLT	emptys into Youngs Bay. *See* OLNEY TOPO
⌖Moro	MOH-roh	SHR	on UPRR abt mid-way btwn Grass Valley and Wasco. Hwy 97
⌖Mosier	MOH-sher	WAS	on Columbia Riv abt 7 mi → of Hood River
⌖Mosquite	muhs-KEET	MAL	on ← bank Snake Riv abt 12 mi ↑ of Ontario
Mount Avery	AY-ver -ee	CUR	elev. 2,030 ft. nr headwaters of Sixes Riv. *See* MOUNT BUTLER TOPO
Mount Billingslea	BIL-ings-lee	CUR/JOE	elev. 4,181 ft. abt 20 mi ne of Kerby
Mount Bolivar	BOH-li-VAHR	COO	elev. 4,319 ft. *See* MT.BOLIVAR YOPO
Mount Elijah	ee-LEYE-juh	JOE	elev. 6,390 ft. *See* GRAYBARK MOUNTAIN TOPO
Mount Gauldy	gawl-dee	TIL	elev. 2,227 ft. *See* HEBO TOPO
Mount Hebo	HEE-boh	TIL	elev. 3,154 ft. *See* HEBO TOPO
Mount Hood	houd	YAM	surprise! This PO was abt 5 mi → of Amity, refers to the "view" of Mt Hood from this site. For "the Mountain Hood," elev. 11,239 ft., in Clackamas Cty, *See* MT HOOD SOUTH TOPO
Mount Isabelle	IS-uh-bel	JKS	elev. 4,494 ft. abt 10 mi ↙ of Gold Hill.*See* MOUNT ISABEL TOPO
Mount Mazama	muh-ZA-muh	KLM	the ancient volcano, estimated to have been about 20,000 ft elev., that blew and left Crater Lake (elev. 6,176 ft.). Elev. at rim abt 8,000 ft. Hwy 62. In this book refer to Crater Lake. *See* CRATER LAKE EAST TOPO

MORO, OR
DEC 16
P M
1985

MOSIER
JAN
16
1906
8 PM
OREGON

MOORHOUSE,
MAY 5 1882
OREGON

MOUNT HOOD
SEP
28
1892
OREG.

69

Mount McLaughlin   mak-LAW-flin   JKS   elev. 9,495 ft. *See* MOUNT
MCLOUGHLIN TOPO

Mount McLoughlin in mid-spring. By the middle of June, the snow has melted. Willow Lake (foreground) part of Willow Lake County Park, a popular camping area, is about 8 miles ⬊ of Butte Falls. —Photo by Bert Webber.

Mount Thielsen   TEEL-suhn   DGL elev. 9,182 ft.

See MOUNT THIELSEN TOPO

Mount Thielsen, on a clear, cold day in mid-winter. The plowed snow banks are about 6 feet high. Camera faces ↗ along Hwy 138 near junction with Hwy 230.

—Photo by Bert Webber

PLACE NAME	PRONUNCIATION	MAP	LOCATION
Mount Pisgah (There are three Mt. Pisgah's in Oregon)	PIZ-gah	WLR	elev. 6,816 ft *See* MOUNT PISGAH TOPO
Mount Popocatepetl	poh-poh-KAT-tuh-pe-ll	LNE	elev. 1,020 ft. *See* GOODWIN PEAK TOPO
Mount Yoran	yohr-ahn	LNE	elev. 7,100 ft. *See* DIAMONE PEAK TOPO
Mowich	moh-wuch	KLM	station on SPRR abt 12 mi ↑ of Chemalt
Mudjekeewis Mtn	muhd-JE-kee-wis	KLM	elev. 6,638 ft. *See* DEVILS PEAK TOPO
Mugwump Lake	muhg-wuhmp	LKE	elev. 4,462 ft. *See* FLAGSTAFF LAKE TOPO
Muir Creek Falls	myoo-er	DGL	elev. 4,360 ft. *See* HAMAKER BUTTE TOPO
Mulino	muh-LEYE-noh	CLK	abt 5 mil ↘ of Canby.
Multnomah	muhlt-NOH-mah	MLT	originally a station on Oregon Electric Ry nr Capitol Hwy and Multnomah Blvd. Now a district in ↙ PDX

[postmark: MULTNOMAH JUN 5 11 AM 1940 OREG.]

PLACE NAME	PRONUNCIATION	MAP	LOCATION
Multorpor Mountain (Butte)	MUHL-tohr-pohr	CLK	elev. 4,646 ft. *See* MOUNT HOOD SOUTH TOPO
Munkers	MUHNK-ers	LIN	abt 3 mi ← of Scio
Munra Point	MUHN-ruh	MLT	elev. 1,760 ft. *See* TANNER BUTTE TOPO
Murphy	MUHR-fe	JOE	abt 6 mi ↓ of Grants Pass. Hwy 238

PLACE NAME	PRONUNCIATION	MAP	LOCATION
Namorf	NAM-ohrf	MAL	abt 10 mi ↙ of Harper
🐟Nansene	nan-seen	WAS	abt 5 mi ↘ of Dufur
Nasoma	nuh-SOH-mah	WAH	station on Oregon Electric Railway trolley-interurban abt 6 mi ↓ of Tigard
🐟Natal	NA-tal	COL	abt 5 mi ↘ of Mist
🐟Natron	NAY-truhn	LNE	station on SPRR on Middle Fort Willamette Riv abt 5 mi ↘ of Springfield
🐟 Naylox	NAY-lahks	KLM	on → side of Klamath ake abt 9 mi ↑ of Klamath Falls
Neacoxie Creek	nee-ah-kahx-ee	CLT	on Clatsop Plains. Its nearby lake was re-named "Sunset Lake" by real estate people. *See* GEARHART TOPO
Neahkahanie Mountain	nee-ah-KAHN-ee	TIL	elev. 1,631 ft. Hwy 101 *See* NEHALEM TOPO
Neawanna	nee-ah-WAN-nah	CLT	within 1 mi of Seaside . *See* GEARHART TOPO
🐟 Necanicum	nee-KAN-i-kuhm	CLT	on Nechicum Riv abt 12 mi ↘ of Seasdide
🐟 Nehalem	ne-HAYL-uhm	TIL	on ← side of riv abt 2 mi → of Manzanita being abt mid-way btwn Manzanita and Wheeler

WILDLIFE CONSERVATION
KING
3¢ UNITED STATES POSTAGE 3¢
NEHALEM DEC 5 3 –PM 1956 OREG.

Nellies Point	NEL-ees	CUR	← of Port Orford. *See* PORT ORFORD OE W TOPO
Nena Creek	NEE-nah	WAS	on Warm Springs Ind. Reser.
🐟 Nenamusa	nee-nam-YOO-suh	TIL	on Nestucca Riv abt 8 mi → of Blaine
🐟 Neotsu	nee-OHT-soo	LIC	on ↓ side of Hwy 101 ↑ of Devils Lake nr Lincoln City
Nesika Beach	nes-kee-kah	CUR	abt mid-way btwn Wedderburn and Ophir. Hwy 101

PLACE NAME	PRONUNCIATION	MAP	LOCATION
 Neskowin	NES-koh-win	TIL	abt 5 mi ↙ of Oretown. Hwy 101

Nesmiths	NES-miths	POK	abt 4 mi ← of Dallas
Nestocton	nes-TAWK-tuhn	TIL	on Tillamook Riv site unclear. *See* biblio for Helbock
Nestucca River	nez-TUHK-uh	TIL/YAM	empties in Pacific Ocean ↓ of Pacific City
Neverstil	never-stil	COL	on Nehalem Riv at confluence with Deep Cr abt 2 mi ↓ of Birkenfeld. *See* TURNER CREEK TOPO
Newell Spring	NYOO-el	JEF	on Madras-Ashood cty road. *See* TELLER BUTTE TOPO
Niagara	neye-AG-ruh	MAR	abt 7 mi → of Mill City
Nice	NEES	LIC	was on Alsea Bay but frequently moved. *See* bibliography for Helbock
Nish	NISH	SHR	station on RR nr Moro
Nofog	NOH-fawg	DGL	abt 12 mi → of Dixonville
Nonpareil	nahn-puh-REL	DGL	on Calapooya Cr abt 7 mi → of Oakland
Noti	NOH-teye	LNE	abt 6 mi ← of Elmira
Nye Beach	n-EYE	LIC	at the beach-front now a district in Newport
Nyssa	NIS-uh	MAL	on Snake Riv btwn Ontario and Adrian. Hwy 201

PLACE NAME	PRONUNCIATION	MAP	LOCATION
🕮Oak	ohk	COO	abt 4 mi → of Bridge on Mioddle Fork Coquille Riv.
🕮Oasis	oh-AY-cis	GIL	abt 4 mi ↗ of Olex in Eightmile Canyon
🕮O'Brien	Oh-BRY-en	JOE	abt 7 mi ↓ of Cave Junction. Hwy 199
🕮Obsidian Cliff	ahb-SID-dee-uhn	LNE	*See* NORTH SISTER TOPO
🕮Oceola	oh-see-oh-la	WAH	abt 1 mi ↓ of Cedar Mill
Ochoco	OH-chuh-koh	CRK	on upper Ochoco Cr abt 1 mi ← of Walton Lk. *See* OCHOCO RESERVOIR TOPO
🕮Odell	oh-DEL	HDR	abt 6 mi ↓ of Hood River on Mt. Hood RR
🕮Odessa	oh -DES-ah	KLM	abt 7 mi ↗ of Lake of the Woods nr ← side of Upper Klamath Lake
Ojalla Bridge (Ojalla is Finnish, does not take the "h" sound of Spanish)	Oh-jal-uh	LIC	tributary of Siletz Riv. *See* MOWREY LANDING TOPO
🕮Olalla	oh-LA-la	DGL	abt 6 mi ↙ of Brockway on Lookingglass Cr.
Olallie Butte	oh-LAHL-lee	MAR	elev. 7,215 ft. btwn Mt. Hood and Mt Jefferson. *See* OLALLIE BUTTE TOPO
🕮Olene	oh-leen	KLM	abt 10 mi ↘ of Klamath Falls. Hwy 140
🕮Olete	oh-LEET	KLM	abt 11 mi ↓ of Bly
🕮Olex	OH-leks	GIL	abt 3 mi ↗ of Mikkalo

PLACE NAME	PRONUNCIATION	MAP	LOCATION
Omro	AHM-roe	LNE	on Siuslaw Riv abt 5 mi ← of Lorane
Ona	OHN-uh	LIC	on Beaver Cr abt 3 mi → of Seal Rock
Oneatta	oh-nee-ET-tuh	LIC	abt 1 mi ← of Winant on Yaquina Riv
Oneonta	oh-nee-AHN-tuh	MLT	on Columbia Riv abt 5 mi ↙ of Warrendale
Ontario	awn-TAYR-ee-oh	MAL	on ← bank of Snake Riv abt 2 mi ↘ of confluence of Malheur Riv
Opal Mountain	OH-pahl	JEF	elev. 5,562 ft. *See* OPAL MOUNTAIN TOPO
Ophir	Oh-fer	CUR	nr mouth of Euche Cr, abt 16 mi ↓ of Port Orford. Hwy 101
Oreana Waterhole	Oh-ree-AN-nuh	HAR	elev. 4,670 ft. *See* MURPHY WATERHOLES NE TOPO
Oregon City	aw-ree-guhn	CLK	on Willamette Riv at falls, across from West Linn

Orenco	ohr-REN-koh	WAH	station on Oregon Electric Ry abt 4 mi → of Hillsboro
Oretech	OHR-TEK	KLM	was on campus of Oregon Institute of Technology, a 4-yr college in Klamath Falls
Oresco	OHR-es-ko	LNE	served the Champion Mine abt 1 mi ↗ of Bohemia

PLACE NAME	PRONUNCIATION	MAP	LOCATION
⏚Oretown	OHR-towhn	TIL	abt 6 mi ↓ of Pacific City. Hwy 101
⏚Orodell	ohr-ah-DEL	UNN	on Grande Ronde Riv in ↗ district of LaGrande
⏚Oroville	OHR-oh-vil	HAR	abt 5 mi ↘ of Fields on a cattle ranch
⏚Orville	OHR-vul	CLK	abt 8 mi ↓ of Barlow
⏚Oswego	ahs-WEE-goh	CLK	name changed in 1961 to

Lake Oswego (city of) surrounds Oswego Lk —formerly called <u>Sucker Lake</u> — nr ← bank Willamette Riv. Hwy 43

⏚Othello	oh-THEL-loh	LNE	site not certain — plausibly on farm on Hwy 99W nr Benton cty line
Outerson Mountain	owt-ter-suhn	MAR	elev. 5,220 ft. *See* MOUNT BRUNO TOPO
Ouxy	OWK-see	KLM	former station on SPRR abt 16 mi ↑ of Klamath Falls. Hwy 97
⏚Owyhee	oh-WEYE-hee	MAL	8 miles ↙ of Nyssa

PLACE NAME	PRONUNCIATION	MAP	LOCATION
Pacard Creek	pa-kerd	LNE	6 mi ↓ of Oakridge
⬧Paisley	PAYS-lee	LKE	abt 10 mi → of Summer Lake

Palanush Butte	PAL-ah-noosh	DES	elev. 5,010 ft.
			See ROUND MOUNTAIN TOPO
⬧Palestine	PAL-uhs-teen	MLT	vicinity of Mt. Tabor
			School in PDX
Palouse Creek	puh-loos	COS	empties into Haynes Inlet
			at ↑ part of Coos Bay. *See* NORTH BEND TOPO
Pamelia Creek	puh-MEEL-yuh	LIN	on ↙ side of Mount
			Jefferson. *See* MOUNT BRUNO TOPO
⬧Parkersburgh	PAHR-kerz-burg	COO	on ↓ side Coquille Riv

abt 3 mi → of Bandon. In WW-II a Japanese bomb-carrying balloon crashed at this site on Mar. 23, 1945. See biblio for *Silent Siege-III*

⬧Parkrose	pahrk-rohs	MLT	district in ↗ PDX entered
			about N.E. 105th and N.E. Prescott
Parrett Mountain	payr-et	YAM	elev. 1,247 ft. → of
			Newberg. *See* NEWBERG TOPO
Parrish Gap	P-AYR-ish	MAR	elev. 519 ft. abt 1 mile

↗ of Marion. *See* TURNER TOPO. *See also* bibliography for *The Oregon Trail Diary of Rev. Edward Evans Parrish in 1844*

Parrott Creek	payr-uht	CLK	flows through New Era.
			See CANBY TOPO
Patawa Creek	pat-uh WA	UMT	*See* PENDLETON TOPO
Patton Valley	PAT-un	WAH/YAM	contains
			Tualatin Riv btwn Gaston and Cherry Grove
⬧Paulina	paw-LEYE -nuh	CRK	on Beaver Cr abt 56 mi
			↘ of Prineville. *See* PAULINA TOPO

78

PLACE NAME	PRONUNCIATION	MAP	LOCATION
Paunia	paw-NEE-uh	KLM	station on SPRR abt 5 mi ↖ of Chemault
⌂Payn	PAY-n	CLK	on ← side of Mt. Scott abt 5 mi ↑ of Clackamas. Hwy I-205
⌂Paynesville	PAYNS-vil	CLK	abt 3 mi ↑ of Sandy ← of Sandy Riv
⌂Pedee	PED-ee	POK	on Luckiamute Riv abt 5 mi ← of Arlie
⌂Pedro	PEE-droh	BKR	at a mine on Pedro Mt. elev. 6,455 ft. *See* MORMON BASIN TOPO
Pelton Dam	PELT-uhn	JEF	on Deschutes Riv 5 mi ↓ of Warm Springs
Pemberton Canyon	pem-ber-tuhn	GIL	elev. 4,146 ft. ↙ of Condon. *See* SHOESTRING RIDGE TOPO
⌂Pendleton	PEND-uhl-tuhn	UMT	on Umatilla Riv. Hwy I-84 *See* PENDLETON TOPO
⌂Pengra	PENG-rah	LNE	station on SPRR abt 1 mi ↓ of Fall Cr. *See* LOWELL TOPO
⌂Peoria	pee-OHR-ee-uh	LIN	on → side of Willamette Riv abt 5 mi ↙ of Shedds
Pernot Mountain	per-nawt	LNE	elev. 3,600 ft. *See* NIMROD TOPO
Perpetua (Cape)	*See* Cape Perpetua		
Petes Point	peets	WAL	elev. 9,675 ft. *See* ANEROID MOUNTAIN TOPO
⌂Philomath	fil OH-muhth	BEN	abt 5 mi ← of Corvallis at junction of Hwy 20/34
Phoca Rock	foh-kah	MLT	nr Bridal Veil. See BRIDAL VAIL TOPO
⌂Phoenix	FEE-nix	JKS	abt 3 mi ↓ of Medford Hwys I-5/ 99

PLACE NAME	PRONUNCIATION	MAP	LOCATION

Phys Point FEYES UNN abt 2 miles ← of Cove.
See COVE TOPO

Pitsua Butte pits-swah DES elev. 5,526 ft. ⬐ of Bend.
See WANOGA BUTTE TOPO

Pisgah (Mountain) *See* Mt. Pisgah

Pistol River PIS-tohl CUR abt 12 mi ↓ of Gold
Beach on the riv. nr the ocean. Hwy 101. PO is in a picturesque roadside store, is classed as a rural station of Gold Beach and carries the Gold Beach ZIP 97444

Placedor Gulch plays-suh-dohr GRT abt 12 mi ↓ of Dayville

⌂**Placer** PLA-suhr JOE PO served the gold miners
on Grave Cr abt 6 mi → of Leland. See bibliography for *Gold Mining in Oregon*

Placidia Butte play-SID-ee-uh HAR elev. 5,513 ft. on ←
edge of cty abt 10 miles ← of Riley

⌂**Plano** play-noh BKR on Burnt River abt 3 mi ⬎
of Durkee btwn Durkee and Weatherby

Plympton Creek PLIM-tuhn CLT at Westport on Columbia Riv

⌂**Pocahontas** pohk-uh-hawnt-uhs BKR elev. 3,673 ft. Way station
on stage coach route abt 7 mi ⬉ of Baker City. *See* WINGVILLE TOPO

⌂**Pokegama** poh-KAY-guh-muh KLM elev. 3,800 ft. at ← end
of Klamath Lake RR abt 38 miles → of Ashland. *See* MULE HILL TOPO

Pollard Butte pohl-luhrd CRK elev. 5,162 ft. *See* POST TOPO

Pompadour Bluff PAWMP-uh-dohr JKS → of Ashland.
See ASHLAND TOPO

⌂**Pondosa** pawn-DOH-sah BKR abt 5 mi ↓ of Medical
Springs just inside Baker Cty. Hwy 203

Popocatepetl *See* Mt. Popocatepetl

⌂**Powwatka** pow-WAT-kuh WAL elev. 3,200 ft. abt 3 mi
⬈ of Promise, abt 2 mi ↓ of Washington line and abt 8 mi ↓ of Troy. *See* TROY TOPO

PLACE NAME	PRONUNCIATION	MAP	LOCATION
Prayl	pray-ul	CLK	station on Oregon Electric Ry at ↓ end of Willamette Riv bridge at Wilsonville
✉Pratum	PPAY-tuhm	MAR	abt 6 mi ↘ of Silverton
✉Preuss	p-roos	COO	PO served miners at SPRR coal mine abt 2 mi ↙ of Coaledo on Beaver Slough
Prevost	pree-vuhst	BKR	station on RR on ← side of Snake Riv now under Brownlee Dam lake abt 7 miles ↑ of Huntington
Priday Agate Beds	PREYE-dee	JEF	abt 15 mi ↗ of Madras on road to Ashwood. *See* bibliography for *Hoffman's Rockhound Gude*
✉Prineville	PREYE-n-vul	CRK	13 mi → of Redmond — at terminal of City of Prineville RR. Hwys 26/126

PLACE NAME	PRONUNCIATION	MAP	LOCATION
Pringle Falls	PRIN-guhl	DES	PO was at the falls on Deschutes Riv abt 10 mi ↖ of LaPine
✉Provolt	PRO-vallt	JKS	abt 4 mi ← of Applegate
Pryor	preye-ohr	LNE	station on SPRR ↘ of Oakridge
Pueblo Mountain	pweb-loh	HAR	↓of Steens Mountain. *See* PUEBLO MOUNTAINS TOPO
✉Pursel	puhrs-uhl	JKS	on Applegate Riv abt 6 mi ↙ of Buncom. *See* bibliography for *Ruch and the Upper Applegate Valley*

81

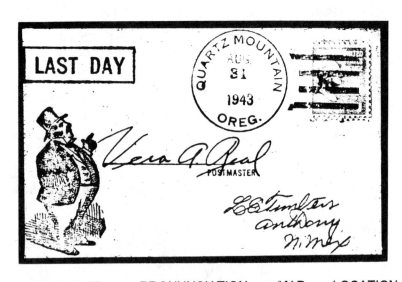

PLACE NAME	PRONUNCIATION	MAP	LOCATION
Quartz Mountain	quahtz	LKE	elev. 6,047 ft. abt 3 mi ↘ of Quartz Mountain Pass. Hwy 140
Quinaby	KWI-nuh-bee	MAR	station on Oregon Electric Ry abt 9 mi ↑ of Salem
Quines Creek	KWEYENS	DGL	abt 11 mi ↓ of Canyonville. Hwy I-5
Quinton	kwin-tuhn	GIL	on UPRR along Columbia Riv abt 6 mi ← of Blalock. Hwy I-84
Quosatana Creek	qwoh-sayt-nah	CUR	See QUOSATANA TOPO

PLACE NAME	PRONUNCIATION	MAP	LOCATION
🕮Rachel	ray-chel	LIN	abt 5 mi ↓ of Sodaville
🕮Ragic	RAJ-ik	CUR	abt 11 mi up (→) Rogue Riv from Gold Beach/Wedderburn

🕮Rajneeshpuram   raj-neesh-PUR-um   WAS on the Antelope - Mitchell cty road nr confluence of Currant and Big Muddy Crs abt 1 mi ← of John Day Riv and 18 mi ↘ of Antelope. The incorporated 1st Class City was at the WAS/JEF cty line but all except one building (clinic) was within Wasco Cty. With as many as 20,000 people at "The Ranch," as it was called," during festivals, the occupants, although entitled to postal service, faced considerable challenges in obtaining a post office. Refer to *The Rajneesh and the U.S. Postal Service* for this episode in bibliography. Rajneesh sannyasins constructed the 90-ft. high, 400 ft. wide Gurdjieff Dam, the largest private-venture reclamation project in Eastern Oregon (no government money), creating Krishnamurti Lake (360,000,000 gallons of water) on which they built a summer resort. Due to population explosion, this innovative, ecologically-sensitive commune planned to construct Rajneeshville on the Jefferson Cty side of the line, but the commune disbanded before this could be done. Refer to bibliography for *Rajneeshpuram, Who Were Its People?* Refer to Antelope in this book. *See also* CLARNO TOPO

Rajneeshpuram is a deserted city (except for resident caretaker), has most of its buildings which are Private Property and Posted. The access road is "public" but there are no services. Cellular phones did not work in June 1994.

PLACE NAME	PRONUNCIATION	MAP	LOCATION
Ramapo	rahm-uh-pough	MLT	See GLADSTONE TOPO
Ramo Flat	ray-moh	UNN	abt 7 mi ⬈ of Union. See UNION TOPO
Rancheria Rock	ranch-uh-REE-ah	WLR	elev. 4,909 ft. See FOSSIL SOUTH TOPO
Raygold	ray-GOHLD	JKS	SPRR corruption of Gold Ray for station nr Gold Ray Dam on Rogue Riv nr Gold Hill abt 2 mi ⬉ of Tolo
Redess	red-es	HAR	cattle ranch abt 14 mi ⬈ of Burns
Redne	red-nee (or, red'n)	MAR	abt 5 mi ← of Detroit
Reichen Well	RIKEN	JEF	elev. 2,775 ft. See BUCK BUTTE TOPO
Reid Glacier	REED	CLK	on ← side of Mount Hood. See MOUNT HOOD SOUTH TOPO
✉Reith	reeth	UMT	station and RR repair shop abt 4 mi ← of Pendleton
✉Reuben	ROO-buhn	COL	on Columbia Riv abt 1 mi ↓ of Goble
Rhea	REE-ah	MOR	abt 7 mi ↓ of Heppner
✉Rhododendron	roh-doh-DEN-druhn	CLK	abt 2 mi ⬈ of Zig Zag. Hwy 26
✉Rickreall	RIK-ree-awl	POK	on Rickreall abt 4 mi → of Dallas. Hwy 99W
✉Riddles	Rid-els	DGL	changed to Riddle. Station on SPRR abt 5 mi ⬉ of Canyonville on Cow Cr
✉Riley	REYE-le	HAR	abt 20 mi ← of Hines. At junction Hwys 20 / 395

PLACE NAME	PRONUNCIATION	MAP	LOCATION
🖾Rieth	reeth	UMT	spelling change from <u>Reith</u>
Robideau Landing	roh-bee-doo	DES	*See* CRANE PRAIRIE RESERVOIR TOPO
🖾Rocca	rahk-uh	POK	abt 6 mi ↙ of Valsetz
Rock Mesa	may-suh	DES	elev. 6,705 ft. *See* SOUTH SISTER TOPO
Rodeo	ROH-dee-oh	HAR	abt 6 mi ↓ of Burns. (The Spanish "roh-DEY-oh" is uncommon here)
🖾Rognes	rohg-nes	WAL	abt 18 mi ↑ of Enterprise
🖾Rogue River	rohg	JKS	name of town and riv. Riv runs through Grants Pass. Hwy I-5
🖾Rolyat	rohl-yat	DES	2 mi → of Hampton but PO moved to Lake Cty in 1919
🖾Rondowa	rahn-DOH-ah	WAL	elev. 2,400 ft. Station at junction on UPRR abt 4 mi ↗ of Palmer Junction. *See* RONDOWA TOPO
Ropers Bunion	ROH-puhrs	JKS	elev. 2,200 ft. *See* ASHLAND TOPO
Rosary Lakes	rohs-ayr-ee	KLM	*See* ODELL LAKE TOPO
Rouen Gulch	ROW-en	BKR	abt 6 mi ← of Baker City. *See* WINGVILLE TOPO
🖾Rowena	ROH-ee-nuh	WAS	station on earlier O.W.R.& N. RR (now UPRR) on Columbia Riv abt 5 mi → of Mosier
Roylat	ROI-laht	DES/LKE	moved several times. Refer to Helbock in biblio
🖾Royston	ROI-stuhn	KLM	elev. 4,940 ft. abt 4 mi → of Yainlex Butte and abt 8 mi ↙ of Bly on the Bonanza Road
🖾Ruch	ROOSH	JKS	abt 7 mi ↙ of Jacksonville. Hwy 238. *See* biblio for *Ruch and the Upper Applegate Valley*
Rudio Mountain	ROO-dee-oh	GRT	elev, 5,498 ft. *See* SHEEP RIDGE TOPO
🖾Rufus	ROO-fuhs	SHR	on Columbia Riv abt 5 mi → of Biggs

PLACE NAME	PRONUNCIATION	MAP	LOCATION
Rujada	roo-ja-doh	LNE	elev. 2,980 ft. abt 6 mi → of

Culp Creek at a logging camp end-of-track on Oregon, Pacific & Eastern Rwy. *See* ROSE HILL TOPO

| Ruthton Point | ROOTH-tuhn | HDR | on Columbia Riv abt 2 mi ← of Hood River |
| Rutledge | RUHT-lej | SHR | abt 5 mi ↘ of Grass Valley |

PLACE NAME	PRONUNCIATION	MAP	LOCATION

Sacajawea Peak   sah-kuh-juh-WEE-uh   WAL elev. 9,839 ft. Although the pronunciation shown has been taught in schools for decades, a re-interpretation yields <u>suh-KOG-uh-way</u>. *See* EAGLE GAP TOPO

⌂**Saginaw**   SAG-i-naw   LNE abt 2 mi ↑ of Cottage Grove. Hwy I-5/99

Sahale Falls   sah-HAH-lee   HDR *See* MOUNT HOOD SOUTH TOPO

⌂**Salado**   suh-LAY-doh   LIC On Elk Cr abt 8 mi ↘ of Toledo

Salene Lake   sa-LEEN   COL nr ← bank of Multnomah Channel ↑ of Scappoose

Saleratus Creek   sal-er-at-tuhs   LNE ↙ of Austa
See CLAY CREEK TOPO

⌂**Salineville**   suh-LEEN-vil   MOR abt 5 mi ↗ of Lexington

⌂**Salisbury**   SAL-is-ber-ree   BKR on Sumpter Valley RR abt 10 ↓ of Baker City.

⌂**Salmonberry**   SAM-uhn-beh-ree   TIL on old Pacific Rwy & Navigation RR (now SPRR) abt 5 mi → of Rector

⌂**Samaria**   sam-MAIR-ee-uh   LNE at Pacific Ocean abt 3 mi ↑ of Heceta Head lighthouse

⌂**Sandlake**   sand-layk   TIL on coast abt 3 mi ↓ of Cape Lookout on Sand Cr near Pacific Ocean. Some maps show the "lake" as a bay but as long as the low dune holds, it is a "lake."

⌂**Sandstone**   sand-stow-n   CUR nr Blacklock Point ↙ of Floras Lake and site of Lakeport 3+ mi ↙ of Langlois. *See* bibliography for *Lakeport, Ghost Town of the South Oregon Coast*

⌂**San Rafael**   raf-el   MLT at 1914 NE 122nd Ave. near San Rafael St. A district of PDX

⌂**Santiam**   SAN-tee-AM   LIN on S.Santiam Riv abt 4 mi ↖ of Sweet Home

⌂**Santyam**   SAN-tee-AM   LIN on land now occupied by City of Lebanon

⌂**Sauvies**   SAW-vee   MLT on → bank of Sauvie Isl at Reeder Point on Columbia Riv. abt 12 mi ↓ of St. Helens

⌂**Scappoose**   skap-POOS   COL on Multnomah Channel ↖ of PDX. Hwy 30

PLACE NAME	PRONUNCIATION	MAP	LOCATION

Schofield Creek SKOH-feeld DGL tributary of Umpqua River at Reedsport. *See* REEDSPORT TOPO

📪Scholls SHOHLZ WAH abt 2 mi ↓ of Tualatin Riv btwn Hillaboro and Newberg

Schott Canyon skaht GIL ↙ of Condon. *See* schott canyon topo

Schreiner Peak SHREYE-ner CLK elev. 5,678 ft *See* BULL OF THE WOODS TOPO

📪Scio SEYE-oh Linn abt mid-way btwn Stayton and Lebanon

📪Scofield SKOH-feeld WAH station on SPRR 3 mi ↑ of Buxton

Sebastian (Cape) *See* Cape Sebastian

Seekseekwa Creek seek-seek-wa JEF elev. 3,450 ft. *See* SHITIKE BUTTE TOPO

📪Seghers SEE-gers WAH station on SPRR abt 2 mi ↑ of Gaston

Selah SEH-luh MAR station on SPRR abt 3 mi ↙ of Silverton

📪Seneca SEHN-ee-kuh GRT on Silves Riv in high meadow btwn Canyon City and Burns abt 25 miles ↓ of Canyon City. Hwy 395

📪Sepanek sep-AHN-eck MOR abt 8 mi ↗ of Lexington.

Serrano Point seh-RAN-oh HAR btwn Alvord Desert and Alvord Lake. Elev. 4,513 ft. *See* ANDREWS TOPO

Seufert soo-fohrt WAS station on RR → of The Dalles

PLACE NAME	PRONUNCIATION	MAP	LOCATION

⌖Shaniko — SHAN-i-koh — WAS 8 mi ↖ of Antelope.Hwy 97

Shasta Costa — SHAS-tuh- KAWS-tuh — CUR tributary of the Rogue River. *See* AGNESS TOPO

⌖Sheaville — SHAY-vil — MAL on Cow Cr abt 1 mi ← of Idaho line abt 12 mi ↑ of Jordan Valley. Hwy 95

Sherars Bridge — SHERZ — WAS elev. 725 ft. abt 8 mi → of Tygh Valley. *See* SHERARS BRIDGE TOPO

⌖Shevlin — SHEV-luhn — DES/KLM a mobile logging camp with PO that moved with the work. Refer to biblio for *Newberry National Volcanic Monument. See also* biblio for Helbock

Shimanek — shim-AWN-ik — LIN One of the newest covered bridges — spans Thomas Creek near Scio

Shitike — shi-TEYEK — JEF elev. 5,080 ft. on ↓ part of Warm Springs Indian Reservation. *See* SHITIKE TOPO

Siboco — seye-boh-koh — LNE station on SPRR on ↓side Siuslaw Riv abt 2 mi ↓of Cushmanabt 6 miles → of Florence

⌖Signal — sig-nul — LNE station on SPRR on Midfork Willamette Riv abt 6 mi ↘ of Lowell

⌖Siletz — si-LETZ — LIC abt 7 mi ↑ of Toledo

Silica — SIL-i-kah — GIL station on RR abt 6 miles ↗ of Arlington

⌖Siltcoos — sil-koos — LNE on SPRR on → shore of Siltcoos Lake 2 mi ↑ of Ada and abt 1 mi ↓ of Canary

⌖Silvies — sil-vees — GRT on Silvies Riv abt 7 mi ↓ of Seneca. Hwy 395

Simax Beach — sim-maks — KLM elev. 4,855 ft. at ↑ end of Crescent Lake. *See* CRESCENT LAKE TOPO

PLACE NAME	PRONUNCIATION	MAP	LOCATION

⌐Simnasho   sim-NASH-oh   WAS abt 10 mi ↓ of
Wapinitia and 14 mi ← of North Junction.

⌐Sinamox   sin-uh-mawks   WAS station on old Oregon
Trunk RR abt 12 mi ↘ of Dufer

⌐Sinemasho   sin-e-MASH-oh   WAS same locality as Simnasho

Sisi Butte   seye-seye   CLK elev. 5,617 ft.
See PINEHEAD BUTTES TOPO

⌐Siskiyou   SIS-kyoo   JKS Was a village for workers
for SPRR at highest point for the RR in the Siskiyou mts. Elev. abt 4,080 ft. Site included east portal of
Tunnel 13 where, on Oct 11, 1923, the three DeAutremont brothers looking for $40,000, blew up the mail
car, killed the train crew and the Post Office Railway Mail Clerk. In bibliography see *Orgon's Great Train
Holdup, Bandits Murder 4—Didn't Get a Dime.* Siskiyou village was dismantled, only trackside shed
remains, is abt ¼-mile ← of Hwy I-5 on a narrow dirt road at Mt. Ashland Exit, abt 4 mi ↑ of California
line. *See* SISKIYOU TOPO

⌐Sitkum   SIT-kuhm   COO abt 5 mi e of Dora on old
wagon road along East Fork of Coquille Riv.

⌐Siuslaw   seye-YOO-slaw   LNE abt 5 mi ↑ of the
present day Lorane. is also name for river. *See* MAPLETON TOPO

**This sign for the "seye-YOO-slaw" Valley Bank is in
Florence on the Oregon coast. Hwy 101.** —Photo by Bert Webber

PLACE NAME	PRONUNCIATION	MAP	LOCATION
⌂Skipanon	SKIP-pa-nuhn	CLT	abt 2 mi ↓ of Warrenton
Skookum Rock	SKOO-kuhm	CRK	*See* OPAL MOUNTAIN TOPO
Skookumhouse Butte	SKOO-kuhm-hows	CUR	elev. 4,185 ft. *See* QUOSANTANA BUTTE TOPO
⌂Skulspring	SKUL-spring	MAL	abt 15 mi → of Creston nr Skull Springs
Slagle Creek	SLAY-guhl	JKS/JOE	elev. 1,440 ft. abt 10 mi ↘ of Grants Pass. *See* GOLDEN TOPO
Sluice Creek Rapids	sloos	WAL	flows into Snake River. *See* OLD TIMER MOUNTAIN TOPO (ID)
Soosap Peak	soo-sap	CLK	elev. 4,681 ft. → of N.Fork Molalla Riv. *See* soosap peak topo
⌂Somerange	SUHM-er-aynje	HAR	PO started on stockman's supply camp on Steens Mt then moved to ranch Hq at what is now Frenchglen
⌂Spicer	SPEYE-ser	LIN	station on narrow-gauge Oregonian RR abt 5 mi ← of Lebanon
⌂Spikenard	SPIK-en-ahrd	JKS	on Evans Cr abt 1 mi ↓ of Asbestos
Staats Creek	stats	BEN	*See* ARLIE SOUTH TOPO
Stahlbusch Island	STAHL-boosh	BEN	*See* RIVERSIDE TOPO
⌂Starvout	STAHR-vow-t	DGL	on Starvout Cr abt 3 mi → of Azalea
⌂Stauffer	STAW-fer	LKE	abt 20 mi ↑of Butte. *See* biblio for Helbock for details
Steinnon Creek	STEE-nuhn	COO	*See* McKINLEY TOPO
Stout Mountain	stowt	MAR	elev. 1,382 ft.*See* stout mountain topo
⌂Straightburg	STRAYT-burgh	HDR	on Neal Cr abt 7 mi ↓of Hood River
⌂Strassel	stra-sel	WAH	station on old Pacific Ry & Navigation Co RR abt 3 mi → of Timber
Stukel Mountain	STOO-kuhl	KLM	elev. 6,525 ft. *See* LOST RIVER TOPO

PLACE NAME	PRONUNCIATION	MAP	LOCATION
Sturtevant Cemetery	STERT-uh -vuhnt	UMT	nr Crow. Elev.
⬤Sublimity	suhb-LIM-i-tee	MAR	2 mi ↑ of Stayton
Sumac Creek	shoo-mak	WAL	nr Chico. *See* ROBERTS TOPO
⬤Sumner	SUHM-ner	COO	abt 8 mi ↑ of Coquille
⬤Sumpter	SUHMP-ter	BKR	elev. 4,480 ft. On North

Powder Riv., site of new Sumpter Valley Dredge State Park. Refer to biblio for *Dredging For Gold*. Abt 27 miles ← of Baker City. Hwy 7/220. *See* SUMPTER TOPO

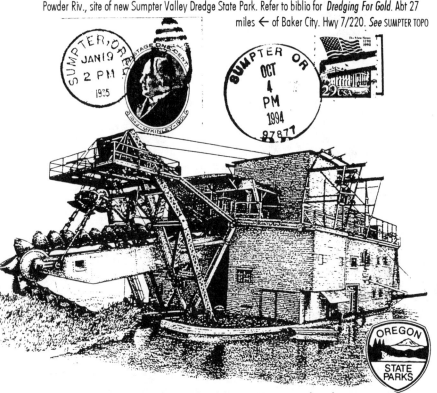

The City of Sumpter, a near-ghost town some say, has been a summer tourist hide-a-way for years. The Oregon State Parks Department is developing a First Class historic mining park in town centered around a huge old gold dredge. Sumpter, about 27 miles west of Baker City, is within the Eastern Oregon historic gold mining area. The town is seeing thousands of new visitors because the weird monster of a dredge will eventually be open for tours. The historic Sumpter Valley Railroad, which operates a short stretch of track nearby, plans to extend its rails to circle the dredge with a passenger station in the park.

Refer to *Dredging For Gold - Documentary* (see biblio) for pictures and details about the Sumpter Valley Gold Dredge. —drawing from Oregon State Parks

PLACE NAME	PRONUNCIATION	MAP	LOCATION
🕮Suntex	suhn-teks	HAR	abt 6 mi ← of Riley
🕮Suplee	SUHP-lee	GRT/HAR	PO moved from place to place. *See* biblio for Helbock
🕮Sutherlin	SUHTH-er-len	DGL	2 mi ↑ of Oakland on Sutherland Cr abt 12 mi ↑ of Roseburg on Old Hwy 99. Hwy I-5
Suttle Lake	SUH-tuhl	JEF	elev. 3,450 ft. abt 14 miles ↖ of the Sisters. Hwy 20.
🕮Suver	soo-ver	C-4	POK station on SPRR abt 3 mi ↑ of Parker
🕮Svensen	SVEN-suhn	CLT	on Columbia Riv abt 8 mi → of Astoria. Hwy 30
Swart	sw-AHRT	UMT	station and PO on RR abt 7 mi ↓ of Gibbon
🕮Sycamore	SIK-uh-mohr	MLT	on Johnson Cr abt 3 mi → of Lents district of PDX
🕮Sylvan	SIL-van	MLT	abt 1 mile ← of Portland Zoological Gardens (Washington Park) and ↑ of Hwy 26

PLACE NAME	PRONUNCIATION	MAP	LOCATION
Taghum Butte	tay-guhm	DES	elev. 6,153 ft.
			See FUZZTAIL BUTTE TOPO
Tahkenitch Lake	TAK-uh-NICH	DGL	elev. 15 ft. abt 6 mi ↑
			of Gardiner. Hwy 101

The Oregon Dunes Recreation Area stretches along Highway 101 south of Florence. —Photo by Bert Webber

✉Takilma	tah-KIL-mah	JOE	abt 4 miles → of O'Brien
Talapus Butte	tal-uh-puhs	DES	elev. 6,158 ft. west of
			Sparks Lake, *See* SOUTH SISTER TOPO
✉Talbot	TAL-buht	MAR	station on Oregon Electric
			Ry abt 12 mi north of Albany and 4 mi s of Ankney
✉Tamarack	TAM-er-ak	UMT	PO on road btwn Elgin
			and Weston abt 8 mi → of Weston

94

PLACE NAME	PRONUNCIATION	MAP	LOCATION
Tangent	TAN-jent	LIN	station on SPRR abt 7 mi ↓ of Albany
Techumtas Island	te-KUHM-tus	UMT	Isl in Columbia Riv → of Umatilla
Tecumseh Creek	tuh-KUM-suh	KLM	abt 1 mi ↑ of Klamath Agency
Tellurium Peak	tel-ler-ee-uhm	DGL	elev. 3,483 ft. *See* CANYONVILLE TOPO
Telocaset	TEL-oh-KA-set	UNN	station on UPRR abt 8 mi ↓ of Union

PLACE NAME	PRONUNCIATION	MAP	LOCATION
Tenasillahe Island	ten-ahs-IL-ah-hee	CLT	*See* CATHLAMET TOPO (WA)
Tenino Creek	te-NEYE-noh	JEFF	*See* WARM SPRINGS TOPO
Terrebonne	TER-uh-bawn	DES	abt 5 mi ↓ of Redmond. Hwy 97
Tethrow Recreation Site	TETH-er-owh	DES	elev. 4,200 ft. *See* PISTOL BUTTE TOPO
Texum	TEX-shum	KLM	abt 3 mi ↙ of Klamath Falls.
Thayer Glacier	thay-er	DES	*See* NORTH SISTER TOPO
The Dalles	DALZ	WAS	on Columbia Riv abt 21 mi

→ of Hood Riv. Hwy I-84. The early community was named Dalles City for the particular rock formation in the Columbia Riv. but was commonly called The Dalles to avoid confusion with "Dallas" in Polk Cty. The name City of The Dalles was officially adopted in June 1966. To add to the confusion, the first name Dallas was changed to "Wascopam" between 1853 and 1860. A few writers argue that The Dalles was the western end of the Oregon Trail. In reality, The Dalles was the point where earliest pioneers sold their wagons then most took to boats in the river to complete their journey to the Willamette Valley. Starting in 1845, The Dalles was a major rest area for pioneers who elected to proceed either by boat or to continue with their wagons on the Barlow Road, around Mt. Hood, directly into the Willamette Valley at Oregon City. Refer to bibliography for *Orgon City (By Way of the Barlow Road) at the End of the National Historic Oregon Trail.*

PLACE NAME	PRONUNCIATION	MAP	LOCATION

Thelake (one word)   thuh-lake   **HAR**   PO was on → side of Mann Lake Ranch abt 10 mi ↙ of Alberson

Theora   thee-oh-ruh   **LKE**   abt 4 mi ← of Goose Lk and abt 1 mi ← of Westside

Thiel Creek   **THEEL**   **LIC**   *See* NEWPORT SOUTH TOPO

Thielson (Mt)   *See* Mount Thielsen

Thurston   thurz-tuhn   **LNE**   abt 3 mi → of Springfield on McKenzie Riv

Tiara   **TEE-aruh**   **HAR**   abt 10 mi ↙ of Frenchglen

Tichenor Rock   **TISH-ner**   **CUR**   at Port Orford. Hwy 101

Tiernan   **TEE-air-nan**   **LNE**   btwn Florence and Mapleton on Siuslau Riv

Tierra del Mar   tee-AIR-uh   **TIL**   abt 4 mi ↑ of Pacific City on coastal county road; one of the better, smoother beaches for finding Japanese glass fishing floats in winter. See biblio for *I'd Rather Be Beachcombing*

Tigard   **TEYE-gerd**   **WAH**   btwn Lake Grove and Beaverton. Hwy 99W

Tillamook   **TIL-uh-muhk**   **TIL**   on ↘ side of Tillamook Bay. Jct Hwys 6/101

Tillamookgate   **TIL-uh-mook-gayt**   **YAM**   abt 1 mi ← of Chesterbrook at crest of ridge on old road the site called the "gateway" to Tillamook

Tillangora Creek   **TIL-ahn-go-ruh**   **CLT**   *See* TILLAMOOK HEAD TOPO

PLACE NAME	PRONUNCIATION	MAP	LOCATION
Tillicum Creek	TIL-i-kuhm	UMT	*See* HURON TOPO
Tipsoo Peak	TIP-soo	DGL	elev. 8,031 ft. *See* MOUNT THIELSEN TOPO
Toketee Falls	TOH-kee-tee	DGL	on N.Umpqua Riv abt 33 mi → of Glide. Hwy 138
Toledo	TOH-lee-doh	LIC	abt 8 mi e→ of Newport
Tolo	toh-loh	JLS	abt 2 mi ↑ of Central Point. Hwys 99 / I-5
Tolovana Park	toh-loh-van-nah	CLT	nr ↓end of Cannon Beach and abt 2 mi ↓ of City of Cannon Beach
Tonquin	TAHN-kwin	WAS	station on Oregon Electric Ry abt 3 mi ↓ of Beaverton
Tou Velle State Park	too-VEL	JKS	on Rogue Riv about 2½ mi downstream from Hwy 62, ← of White City
Trask	trask	TIL	two sites on Trask Riv for discontinued PO. See biblio for Helbock
Trece	trees	WAH	abt 5 mi ↘ of Beaverton
Treharne	TRE-hehrn	COL	abt 2 mi ↓ of Vernonia
Tremont		MLT	abt 1 mi ↗ of Woodstrock nr present SE 70th St and Foster Rd
Trenholm	tren-holum	COL	on Milton Cr 8 mi ← of Columbia City
Tsiltcoos	see: Siltcoos		
Tualatin	too-WAHL-uh-tuhn	WAH	↘ of Beaverton. Hwy I-5

97

PLACE NAME	PRONUNCIATION	MAP	LOCATION
🖃Tule Lake	too-lee	KLM	abt 4 mi → of Malin nr ↑ edge of Tule Lake (also known as Rhett Lake)
🖃Tumalo	TUHM-uh-loh	DES	nr Bend. The PO had 2 sites. In biblio see Helbock
Tumalt Creek	too-mawlt	MLT	*See* MULTNOMAH FALLS TOPO
Tutuilla Creek	toh-toh-ilah	UMT	*See* PENDTETON TOPO
Tututni Pass	too-too-nee	KLM	*See* MAKLAKS CRATER TOPO
🖃Twickenham	TWIK-en-ham	WLR	on ↑ side of John Day R abt 12 mi ↑ of Mitchell
Tycer Creek	TEYE-ser	JOE	abt 5 mi ↘ of Kerby
🖃Tyee	tye-ee	DGL	abt 7 mi ↓ of Kellogg
🖃Tygh Valley	teye	WAS	abt 17 mi ↓ of Dufer. Hwy 197

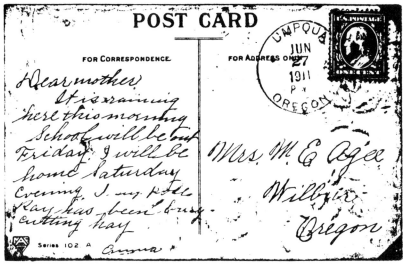

PLACE NAME	PRONUNCIATION	MAP	LOCATION
Ukiah	yoo-KEYE-uh	UMT	abt 76 mi ↓ of Albee on Camas Cr. Hwy 234
Uvalstad	you-VAHL-stad	JKS	abt 4 mi ← of Persist being abt 14 mi ↗ of Trail
Umapine	yoo-muh-peyen	UMT	abt 8 mi ↖ of Milton-Freewater and abt 2 mi ↓ of Washinton line.
Umatilla	yoo-mah-TIL-uh	UMT	on Columbia Riv abt 9 mi → of Irrigon. Jct of Hwys 730 / I-82
Umli	UHM-lee	KLM	elev. 4,730 ft. Believed to be name of spur or siding on private RR just → of SPRR mainline, See CRESCENT LAKE TOPO
Umpqua	UHMP-kwaw	DGL	on Umpqua Riv abt 7 mi ← of Sutherland. There was an Umpqua City on bank near the river's mouth then the PO moved across river to the sand spit to serve Fort Umpqua of which there is no present trace
Unavilla	uhn-uh-VIL-uh	CLK	abt 2 mi ↑ of Sandy on ↑ bank of Sandy Riv.
Union	yoon-yuhn	UNN	abt 12 mi ↘ of LaGrande. Hwys 203 / 237
Utopia	yoo-TOH-pe-uh	WAL	abt 2 mi ↘ of Promise

99

PLACE NAME	PRONUNCIATION	MAP	LOCATION
☞Valfontis	val-PHON-tis	POK	on ← bank of Willamette Riv
☞Vannoy	van-noi	JOE	abt 5 mi w of Grants Pass on Vannoy Cr nr confluence with Applegate Riv.
☞Vanora	van-OHR-uh	JEF	abt 3 mi → of Warm Springs on → bank of Deschutes Riv
☞Vansycle	van-seye-kel	UMT	abt 6 mi ↖ of Helix. A station with PO on Northern Pac RR in Vancycle canyon
Veatch	vech	LNE	abt 3 mi ↙ of Cottage Grove
Veazie Creek	vee-zee	CRK	*See* CADLE BUTTE TOPO
☞Venator	va-NAT-er	HAR	abt 13 mi → of Princeton but moved several times
☞Veneta	ve-NEE-tah alternate: <u>ven-EE-tah</u>	LNE	abt 1 mi ↓ of Elmira on Long Tom Riv
☞Verboort	ver-BOORT	WAH	abt 2 mi ↗ of Forest Grove
Verdure	VERD-er	LIN	12 mi ↙ of Albany
☞Vernie	VEHR-ne	MAL	abt 6 mi ↑ of Ontario
☞Vernonia	ver-NOHN-ee-uh	COL	at confluence of Rock Cr and Nehalem Riv abt 19 mi ←of St.Helens
☞Vesper	ves-pur	CLT	in Nehalem Valley nr county line abt 6 mi ↙ of Mist
☞Vida	VEYE-duh	LNE	abt 6 mi → of Leaburg
☞Viento	ve-EN-toh	HDR	on Columbia Riv. A station on UPRR abt 7 mi ← of Hood Riv
Vingie Creek	vin-gee	LIC	*See* YACHATS TOPO
☞Viola	veye-OH-luh	CLK	abt 3 mi ← of Estacada
☞Vistillas	vis-TIL-uhs	LKE	started PO in Klamath Cty abt 15 mi ↘ of Bly but moved abt 3 mi → across line
Voorhies	VOHR-hees	JKS	freight siding at Voorhies Orchard on SPRR abt 1½ mi ↖ of Phoenix. Hwy 99 at Stage Rd South

PLACE NAME	PRONUNCIATION	MAP	LOCATION

🕮Waconda   waw-KAHN-duh   MAR two sites for PO the first abt 1 mi ↓ of Gervis where Hwy 99E crossed an old road that connected St.Louis and Parkersburg. Second PO was at station on Oregon Electric RR abt 4 mi ↙ of first site. Both the PO and the RR now gone. *See* GERVIS TOPO

Wahanna Lake   wah-nuh   LNE ↑ of Waldo Lk.
See WALDO MOUNTAIN TOPO

Wahkeena Falls   wah-KEEN-uh   MLT *See* BRIDAL VEIL TOPO

Wahtum Lake   wah-tum   HDR elev. 3, 732 ft.
See WAHTUM LAKE TOPO

🕮Wallamette   wahl-uh-met   CLK variance on spelling of Willamette, as often occurred in early days. PO was in the postmaster's house abt 1 mi ← of Wilsonville. *See also* Williamette

Wakonda   wah-KAHN-duh   LIC village ← of Waldport.
See WALDPORT TOPO

Walcott Tunnel   WAHL-kaht   WAH abt 6 mi ← of Buxton.
See TIMBER TOPO

Wallalute Falls   WAHL-uh-loot   HDR on ↗ slope of Mt. Hood.
See MOUNT HOOD NORTH TOPO

Wallinch   wahl-IN-ch   PLK *See* AIRLIE NORTH TOPO
alternate pron: WAWL-inch

Wallooskee River   wahl-OOS-ke   CLT ↘ of Youngs Riv.
See ASTORIA TOPO

🕮Wallowa   wahl-AH-wa   WAL PO moved three times eventually to present city. For details see biblio for Helbock. *See also* WALLOWA TOPO

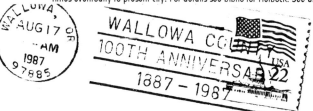

🕮Waluga   wahl-OO-guh   CLK PO at station on SPRR at ← end of Oswego Lk abt where Lake Grove is today. Also, Waluga Jr. High Sch nearby, where editor was school librarian 1965-69

🕮Wamic   WAM-ik   WAS elev. 1,700 ft. on Threemile Cr abt 5 mi ← of Tygh Valley. For PO refer to Tygh Valley. *See* WAMIC TOPO

PLACE NAME	PRONUNCIATION	MAP	LOCATION
⌂Wampus	wahm-puhs	KLM	elev. 3,897 ft. on Klamath Riv abt 3 mi ↑ of Topsy. *See* CHICKEN HILLS TOPO
Wanoga Butte	wan-OH-guh	DES	elev. 5,697 ft. abt 8 mi ↘ of Bachelor Butte. *See* WANOGA BUTTE TOPO
⌂Wapata	WAH-puht-uh	YAM	abt 2 mi ↗ of Cove Orchard
⌂Wapatoe	WAH-puh-tow	WAH	station on SPRR abt 7 mi ↓ of Forest Grove
⌂Wapinitia	wah-pi-NISH-uh	WAS	elev. 2,028 ft. on Wapinitia Cr abt 10 mi ↙ of Maupin. *See* WAPINITIA TOPO
⌂Wasco	WAHS-ko	WAS	abt 1 mi ↓ of Boyd on Fifteenmile Cr
⌂Wascopam	WAHS-ko-pahm	WAS	*See* The Dalles
⌂Wastina	was-TEEN-uh	LKE	abt 7 mi ↙ of Fort Rock
Waucoma Ridge	wah-KOM-uh	HDR	*See* WAHTUM LAKE TOPO
⌂Wauna	WAW-nah	CLT	on Columbia Riv abt 3 mi ↖ of Westport
⌂Wecoma	we-koh-muh	LIC	just ↑ of Lincoln City coast. Hwy 101
⌂Wedderburn	WEHD-der-bern	CUR	on the ↑ bank of the Rogue Riv across from Gold Beach. Hwy 101
⌂Weekly	week-lee	DGL	abt 4 mi ↖ of Tenmile
⌂Welches	WEL-chez	CLK	abt 2 mi ↘ of Wemme on Salmon Riv. Hwy 26
⌂Wemme	WEM-ee	CLK	3 mi → of Brightwood. Hwy 26

PLACE NAME	PRONUNCIATION	MAP	LOCATION

Wenaka — we-NAH-kah — WAL — elev- 3,160 ft- on Grande
Ronde Riv abt 6 mi ← of Promise. Original spelling used "h." PO changed it to "k." *See* DEEP CREEK TOPO

Wendling — when-dling — LNE — abt 15 mi ↗ of Springfield
on Mill Cr.

Weyerhaeuser — WAYR-how-zer — KLM — Timber operations
throughout the Pac.NW. This mill recently closed. All development, including RR, at Bly, removed

Whelpley — WELP-ple — JKS — abt 2 mi ↑ of Leeds abt
7 mi ↙ of Prospect

Wicopee — wik-kuh-pee — LNE — elev. 2,600 ft. station on
SPRR ↘ of Oakridge. See McCREDIE SPRINGS TOPO

Wickiups — WIK-ee-yuhps — DES — campground on Deschutes
Riv ↓ of Crane Prairie. For details, refer to McArthur in biblio

Wilark — WIL-arhk — COL — PO served a timber
company with 2 sites. The final spot was abt 2 mi ↓ of Pittsburg but business was all over by 1945

Wilhoit — WIL-hoyt — CLK — abt 7 mi ↓ of Mololla

Wilksboro — WILKS-bor-roh — WAH — abt I mi ↘ of Banks

Willakenzie — wil-ah-KEN-zee — LNE — district in Eugene abt 3
mi ↑ of city center

Willamette — wil-AM-uht — CLK — on ← bank of Willamette
Riv abt 2 mi ↙ of Hwy I-205 bridge. *See also* Wallamette

Willamina — wil-luh-MEYE-nuh — YAM/POK — PO moved about.
Details are provided by McArthur in biblio

Wimer — wh-EYE-muhr — JKS — 7 mi ↑ of Rogue River

Winant — weye-nant — LIC — on original Corvallis and
Eastern RR (now SPRR) on ↑ bank Yaquina Riv abt 2 mi ↓ of Yaquina

103

West Woahink is one of several recreation areas within Honeyman State Park. The park includes a large overnight camping area. Access is from Highway 101 a few miles south of Florence. —Photo by Bert Webber

Winchuck	win-chuk	CUR	nr mouth of Winchuck Riv mere yards ↑ of Calif. line
Winino	win-EE-noh	LNE	on Middle Fork of Willamette Riv at McCredie Springs abt 10 mi ↙ of Oakridge
Winona	win-OH-nah	JOE	abt 4 mi ↗ of Merlin on Jump Off Joe Cr
Woahink Lake	who-hink	LNE	elev. 38 ft. *See* FLORENCE TOPO
Wocus	WOH-kuhs	KLM	8 mi ↑ of Klamath Falls. Hwy 97
Wrentham	wren-them	WAS	elev. 1,000 ft. abt 6 mi ↓ of Celilo on Fifteenmile Cr. *See* EMERSON TOPO

PLACE NAME	PRONUNCIATION	MAP	LOCATION
Yach	yahoch	TIL	on Little Destucca Riv abt 3 mi ↖ of Dolph
Yachats	yah-hahts	LIC	at the coast at mouth of Yachats Riv. Hwy 101
Yainax	YAH-naks	KLM	PO moved about, became station on California & Eastern RR when name changed to Sprague River. See SPRAGUE RIVER EAST TOPO
Yakso Falls	YAK-sew	DGL	See QUARTZ MOUNTAIN TOPO
Yamada	yah-MAH-dah	LIC	abt 3 mi ↑of Alsea Bay and ↓ mi s of Ona
Yamhill	YAM-hill	YAM	on Yamhill Riv 4 mi ↑ of Carlton. Hwy 240 / 47
Yankton	yahnk-ton	COL	abt 5 mi ← of St. Helens
Yamsay	yam-say	KLM	elev. 4,640 ft. PO at logging camp abt 5 mi ↑ of Yamsay Mt ant abt 20 mi ↗ of Kirk. (Should not be confused with Yamsay station on SPRR a few miles away.) See MAZAMA TOPO
Yaquina	yuh-KEEN-uh	LIC	on ↓shore of Yaquina Bay abt 3 mi ↘ of Newport
Yoakum	YOH-kuhm	UMT	on Umatilla Riv abt 10 mi ↘ of Echo
Yocum	YOH-kuhm	LKE	abt 20 mi ↙ of Lakeview close to California line
Yoncalla	yahn-KAHL-uh	DGL	on Elk Cr abt 5 mi ↘ of Drain. Hwy 99
Yonna	YAH-nuh	KLM	abt 4 mi ↗ of Dairy
Yoran Mountain	yohr-uhn	LNE	elev. 7,100 ft. ↑ of Diamond Peak. See DIAMOND PEAK TOPO
Youtlkut Butte	YOWT-el-kuht	LKE	elev, 5,895 ft. ↓ of Paulina Mts. See INDIAN BUTTE TOPO

For "Z"
Turn to
Page 106

PLACE NAME	PRONUNCIATION	MAP	LOCATION
Zena	ZHEE-nah alternate pron: zehn-nah	POK	abt 7 mi ↖ of Salem on Spring Valley Cr. *See* AMITY TOPO
Zibe Dimmick Park	zeyeb dim-mik	HDR	abt 15 mi ↓ of Hood River. *See* PARKDALE TOPO
Ziebart Reservoir	ZHEE-bahrt	LIN	elev. 820 ft. *See* JORDAN TOPO
Zig Zag	zig-zag	CLK	abt 2 mi ↖ of Rhododendron. Hwy 26
Zion	zeye-un	LNE	abt 4 mi ↓ of Dexter
Zollner Creek	zohl-ner	MAR	↖ of Mt.Angel. *See* SILVERTON TOPO
Zosel Hill	zow-zel	MAR	elev, 624 ft. abt 5 mi ↙ of Salem. *See* SALEM WEST TOPO
Zuckerman Island	ZOO-kehr-mun	KLM	high ground in Lower Klamath Lk nr Worden. *See* WORDEN TOPO
Zumwalt	ZOOM-wahlt	WAL	elev. 215 ft. abt 8 mi ↖ of Imnaha on a twisty county road. *See* ZUMWALT TOPO
Zurfluhs Ponds	zuhr-flufs	LIN	*See* JORDAN TOPO

Bibliography

Barklow, Irene. *From Trails to Rails: The Post Offices, Stage Stops, and Wagon Roads of Union County, Oregon [with Wallowa County Post Offices]*.Enchantments Pub. Co. Enterprise, Ore. 1987.

Black, John and Marguerite. *RUCH and the Upper Applegate Valley.* Webb Research Group. 1990.

Brinlow, George F. *Harney County Oregon, and its Range Land.* Binford & Mort. 1951.

Culp. Edwin D. *Stations West; The Story of Oregon Railways.* Caxton. 1970.

Garrett, Stuart G. *Newberry National Volcanic Monument.* Webb Research Group. 1991.

Geographic Names System (Oregon). Branch of Geographic Names, U. S. Geological Survey [unfinished] Dec. 1992.

Hald, Chris. *Camp White Oregon; The 91st (Fir Tree) Infantry Division.* Webb Research Group. 1994.

Helbock, Richard W. *Oregon Post Offices 1847 - 1982.* LaPosta. 1982.

Hoffman, Charles S. *Hoffman's Rockhound Guide.* (Expanded Ed.) Webb Research Group. 1993.

Labbe, John T. *Fares, Please Those Portland Trolley Years.* Caxton. 1982.

McArthur, Louis L. *Oregon Geographic Names.* (6th Ed.) Oregon Hist. Society. 1992.

Miller, Emmas G. *Clatsop County, Oregon; A History.* Binford & Mort. 1958.

Oregon; End of the Trail. [American Guide Series W.P.A.] Binford & Mort. 1940.

Parrish, Edward Evans. *The Oregon Trail Diary of Rev. Edward Evans Parrish in 1844.* Webb Research Group. 1988.

Webber, Bert. *Dredging For Gold.* Webb Research Group. 1994.

_____. *Gold Mining in Oregon.* Webb Research Group. 1995.

_____. *The Rajneesh and the U.S. Postal Service.* Webb Research Group. 1988.

_____. *Rajneeshpuram: Who Were Its People?* Webb Research Group. 1990.

_____. *Silent Siege-III. Japanese Attacks On North America in World War II, Ships Sunk, Air Raids, Bombs Dropped, Civilians Killed.* Webb Research Group. 1992.

—Continued on next page

Webber, Bert and Margie Webber. *Battle Rock, the Hero's Story.* Webb Research Group. 1992.

_____. *Bayocean, The Oregon Town That Fell Into the Sea.* Webb Research Group. 1989.

_____. *I'd Rather Be Beachcombing.* Webb Research Group. 1993.

_____. *Lakeport, Ghost Town of the South Oregon Coast.* Webb Research Group. 1990.

_____. *Oregon Covered Bridges.* Webb Research Group. 1991. Expanded Ed 1995.

_____. *Oregon City (By Way of the Barlow Road) at the End of the National Historic Oregon Trail.* Webb Research Group. 1993.

_____. *Oregon's Great Train Holdup, Bandits Murder 4, Didn't Get a Dime.* Webb Research Group. 1988.

United States Coast Pilot; Pacific Coast, California, Oregon.... (18th Ed.) U.S. Dept of Commerce. 1982.

About the Author

Bert Webber plays with
the Southern Oregon
Symphonic Band

Bert Webber writes books about what he calls "the fantastic Oregon country." He has written over fifty non-fiction books on subjects relating to nearly every region of the state and says he has only "scratched the surface for there is no shortage of Oregon subjects."

Webber has always been fascinated with the pronunciations of place names. This is because of his wide association with people from around the nation and his having lived in a variety of places.

While Bert Webber was the Librarian at Waluga Junior High School, Lake Oswego, in the late 1960's, he was often called upon for proper pronunciations. For the benefit of the 8th grade social studies teachers, he made a simple list of the most commonly mis-pronounced Oregon place names that were being encountered in Northwest History classes. The list grew, with contribuitions from various sources (see bibliography), to eventually become this book.

Bert has a degree from Whitworth College in journalism, then earned the Masters Degree in Library Science with studies at Portland State University and the University of Portland. He is listed in *Who's Who in the West, Who's Who in the World,* and in *Contemporary Authors.* He was awarded the *Degree of Merit* in *Men of Achievement* in the International Biographical Centre, Cambridge, England.

For fun, he plays Euphonium in the Southern Oregon Symphonic Band, where he also serves on the Board of Control.

He, and his wife, Margie, who is co-author for a number of these books, have lived throughout the Pacific Northwest for many years and specifically in Oregon the last thirty of them. They have four children, all of whom know how to pronounce Oregon place names, and eight grand children who probably do not stand much of a chance of saying any of them wrong either.